U.S. 50
THE FORGOTTEN
HIGHWAY

BY WENDELL TROGDON

A Sentimental Journey
FROM WASHINGTON TO ST. LOUIS

Backroads Press
P.O. Box 651
Mooresville, IN 46158

ISBN 0-9642371-6-4

Cover by Gary Varvel

Pictures by Fabian Trogdon

Maps from Department of Transportations Illinois, Indiana,
Ohio, Virginia, West Virginia

Printed by Country Pines Printing
Shoals, Indiana

DEDICATION

To my wife, Fabian, who was my companion
on U.S. 50 as she has been on the journey
through life for 45 years.

OTHER BOOKS BY WENDELL TROGDON

NOSTALGIA BOOKS

Those Were the Days

Through the Seasons

Carved in Memory

The Country Bumpkin Gang

TRAVEL

Backroads Indiana

Borderline Indiana

Indiana General Stores

BIOGRAPHY

Out Front: The Cladie Bailey Story

BASKETBALL

No Harm/No Foul: Referees are People, Too

Gym Rats: Sons Who Play for Fathers Who Coach

Shooting Stars: Trek to a Championship

Basket Cases: High School Basketball Coaches

Whistle Blowers: A No Harm No Foul Sequel

Damon - Living a Dream (Co-authored with Damon Bailey)

For more information about these books
P.O. Box 651, Mooresville IN 46158
E-mail: wend@iquest

CONTENTS

IN GRATITUDE

We are grateful for the cooperation we received from dozens of people who helped make this book possible. We thank the state, city and town officials who talked with us and responded to our requests for information.

We appreciate the courtesy of the folks along the the route who took time to share their views and to answer our questions. And we acknowledge those who shared their thoughts through e-mail messages and telephone conversations.

The friendliness of those we meet and those with whom we talked will not be forgotten. Our thanks to each of you.

AN OVERVIEW

"Life has taken on the character of a superhighway. In the old days, it took twice as long to get from one town to another, but it was interesting; the drive was interesting. You had to have a little skill to negotiate some of the curves and the turns, and it was intimate."

- Norman Mailer (from a newspaper interview)

U.S. 50 was born in the footprints of George Washington and it has deviated little from the path he mapped across Virginia and what later would be West Virginia to the Ohio River.

It is not an interstate, even today. It is, instead, still interesting, a two-lane journey through an America missed by those seeking the quickest drive between two points. And it takes the skill of an attentive driver to negotiate the twists, turns, steep declines and sharp rises as the road snakes across a section of America most travelers never see.

And U.S. 50 is still intimate, enough so to allow visitors to share the joys and heartaches of the folks who live along the route.

Unlike the interstates, U.S. 50 is not a concrete or asphalt four-lane divided pad to a destination. It is not a fast route to a distant point. It is a slow passage through mountains, farms and small towns, a journey past plantation type mansions and double-wide mobile homes.

It is a drive through the pages of history. It is what "Time Magazine" called "The Backbone of America." It is a view of America beyond the large cities and sprawling suburbs. It is a return to places that remain much as they have for 70 years.

Old towns along the route are worth a visit, not a nod at a "reduce speed limit" and the anticipation of a "resume speed" sign. These are places to park, relax, stroll past stores only a sidewalk width from the road, and for strangers to be greeted as friends.

And there is scenery and history.

In Virginia, the Shenandoah Valley reflects both its beauty and its significant to the birth - and life - of the nation. Horsemen, garbed in expensive riding gear, await fox hunts to come, a reflection of the wealth in the area.

In West Virginia, a sky of blue accentuates the greenery of a million trees that rise and fall over the hills as they grow into mountains. The hills are for squirrel hunters for there are few fox chases by prominent personalities aboard expensive steeds. Towns - such as Romney and Clarksburg - are steeped in history and reminders of war.

A tip of Maryland bisects a small section of West Virginia, causing some residents to feel apart from their fellow statesmen far away in Ocean City and Annapolis.

In southern Ohio, fall comes, cutting crisply into the terrain, turning green into a multitude of colors more decorative than those on an artist's palette. Athens, Chillicothe, Hillsboro and other towns are eager to share their contributions in the development of a nation.

In southern Indiana, winter nears and smoke lifts from wood stoves to disappear into cool looking clouds. Along U.S.50 are Vincennes and its George Rogers Clark Memorial; Bedford and its limestone industry, Seymour, the site of the Reno Brothers who introduced railroad robbery to the American crime scene.

In southern Illinois, Little Cairo it is called, pumps nod endlessly as they bring crude oil from the bowels of the earth. At the courthouse in Salem, a metal detector checks for weapons, a deterrent to crime William Jennings Bryan never dreamed would be needed in his home town.

It is a highway that could be called the heartbeat of a nation. On maps, the route rises and falls raggedly, like lines on a monitor in a hospital's cardiac ward. The road twists trough hairpin turns, follows rivers and railroads, seeks paths of least resistance as it crosses America from Ocean City, Md., to San Francisco.

We have limited this book to that section from Washington to St. Louis for that is the route we know best.

We traveled the highway in two segments, which is how we have decided to relate our experiences. We start those trips at U.S. 50 and Interstate 65 in Seymour, Ind., an intersection called the crossroads of Southern Indiana.

Part I takes us east on U.S. 50 to Washington, Part II west to St. Louis.

Join us now on this sentimental journey as we travel "The Forgotten Highway," recalling the trips of our youth and recording our observations of the present.

PART I

QUOTABLE

"This IS Versailles. It is where most people meet." - Two men at a McDonald's Restaurant in Versailles, Ind.

————————

"I quit smoking. I quit drinking. I quit gambling. I quit hunting. I quit fishing. When I quit working I had to find something else to do. - An antique collector in Addyston, Ohio.

————————

"That's Keeton with an 'e.' You don't get to spell it with an 'a' until you're rich." - A man near Fayetteville, Ohio.

————————

"U.S. 50 is the biggest little highway left in America." - A storekeeper in Rainsboro, Ohio.

————————

"This is a very pleasant community. Its greatest assets are its people." - Mayor Jimmy Colombo, Parkersburg, W.Va

————————

"We can stay here all night if you have the time." - A man at an old jail being converted into a historical museum in West Union, W. Va.

CHAPTER 1

INDIANA
EAST FROM SEYMOUR

We are the roads we take, the stops we make along the way, the people we meet, the lands we visit, the monuments we see, the history we relive. We are a part of yesterday, a slice of today. We are a piece of tomorrow in what we leave along the way.

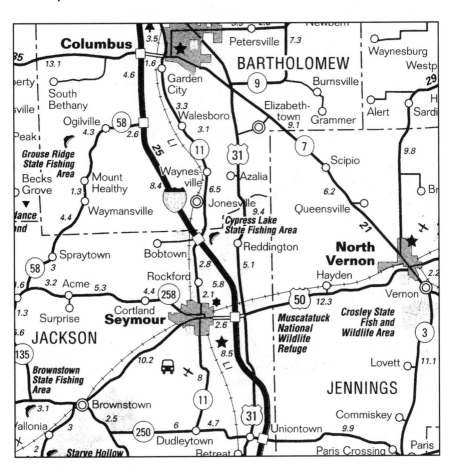

JACKSON COUNTY

It didn't mean much at the time, that report in the "Seymour (Ind.) Tribune" back on August 8, 1917.

Automobiles were still luxuries, not necessities. Most rural folks still traveled on horseback or in buggies and wagons. It likely was difficult for them to realize the significance of the news:

Two major highways would intersect at Seymour, one to be named U.S. 31, which would be a north-south route, the other designated U.S. 50, which would be an east-west road from Lawrenceburg near the Ohio border through North Vernon, Seymour, Brownstown, Vallonia and Medora on its eventual way to Vincennes.

"The two roads will make Seymour the crossroads of southern Indiana . . . if not the nation," the newspaper proclaimed.

U.S. 50 remains, eight decades later, the major highway across south central Indiana, its route changing little along the way from Seymour to Lawrenceburg. Joseph E. Kernan, Indiana's lieutenant governor, calls it "one of the premiere highways in the United States, the only federal east-west road in Indiana south of U.S. 40."

U.S. 50, he notes, is essential to commerce and industry, especially to the many small communities across southern Indiana.

U.S. 31, long since relocated to bypass Seymour, has been bypassed itself, its route for motorists superseded by Interstate 65.

At the east edge of Seymour U.S. 50 crosses under I-65 - a Louisville-Indianapolis connector - before intersecting with U.S. 31 where the traffic flow is controlled by a stoplight.

We remember earlier journeys on U.S. 50 as we begin our drive: Trips east to Washington, D.C. Outings to old Crosley Field in Cincinnati to see the Reds play baseball. Visits to historic Vernon and other eastern Indiana towns.

But this is now, the late 1990s, not the 1940s of our youth.

"Mutton Creek Road," proudly, not sheepishly, says a sign at an entrance to a newer housing development. Up ahead a sign

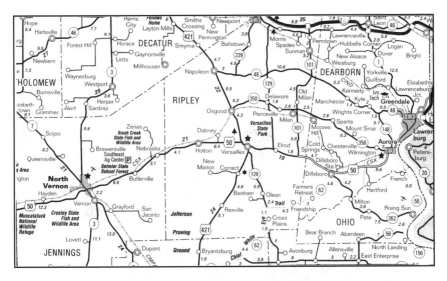

tells us U.S. 50 is the Blue Star Memorial Highway, a tribute to the nation's veterans.

Off to the south astraddle the Jackson-Jennings County line is the Muscatatuck National Wildlife Refuge. Built by the government, it is a memorial to volunteers who formed the Muscatatuck Wildlife Society and help operate the Visitor's Center.

We are in no hurry. It is an ideal fall day, a perfect time to walk the refuge's Chestnut Ridge Trail where black bear, bobcat and wolves once wandered. Tulip and oak trees stretch skyward near wetlands that now attract water fowl. Woodchuck burrows are in the banks of streams near plants such as arrowhead, lizard-tail, cattail and blue flag iris.

White-tail deer, again populous in the area, have formed their own winding trails through the land, which has been restored - through nature and wildlife management - from farm fields and pastures.

The efforts of the volunteers have been rewarded by visitors from Arizona to Germany, who signed the guest book at the Visitors Center and added notes of appreciation for what they have seen.

JENNINGS COUNTY

We enter Jennings County, said to be the only Jennings County in America, near the wildlife refuge. The road is two-lane, undivided, as it stretches toward the east past farms, auto lots and a few businesses that prefer rural rather than urban locations.

There are few reminders of the road's earlier years. That changes when the road drops over a rise.

A view of J.J.'s Corner Store near Hayden

An old-time filling station is at the corner of one of two entrances into Hayden, a small town off to the north of U.S. 50. A roof extends over one bay to the gasoline pumps, the outer drive uncovered. It is an appearance that has remained unchanged, since the station was built at least 70 years ago.

J.J.'s Corner Store it is called. "Gas, sandwiches, groceries. Open 7 days a week," a sign says. It's a convenience for those who travel a highway that doesn't close on Sundays or holidays.

A delivery driver carries fresh bakery items into the store, where groceries, oil and snacks are for sale. So are sandwiches, such as egg and sausage in the morning, ham and other choices at lunch, most for $1.50 each.

At work for owner Randy Johnson is Sue Jackson. "Feel free to look around," she says. The place is larger than it looks, big enough for some former owners to make their home, run the store and raise families.

Floors are old, tongue-in-groove, embedded with the footprints of former owners with names like Andy Eder, the Marshalls and the Maples.

Helping Mrs. Jackson is her granddaughter, Kristen McClain. She is counting soft drinks to be placed in the machines outside. Kristen is too young to attend school, but not too young to learn to count.

And the store is a good place for her to learn about America from local folks, who drop in each day, and from travelers, who stop in for refreshments and to ask directions to their destinations.

It's a place that hasn't changed much for seven decades although the world around it has.

We drive into Hayden and revisit Maschino's Market, a store Sarah Maschino operates in a 140-year-old landmark. Across a corner of the intersection is the town post office, its building not much larger than a postage stamp. Not far away is the Hayden Historical Museum that Rodger Ruddick and his Little Hoosiers, a group of young historians, opened in 1990 to give residents a better idea of the heritage of the area.

Next door to the museum, former Indiana Gov. Edgar Whitcomb lives a peaceful life away from the fanfare of politics. The Whitcomb family home, a modest frame structure, is far from the governor's mansion and political intrigue back in Indianapolis, the state capital.

A modern elementary school has replaced the old high school, which closed in 1960 when students were sent to North Vernon. It was the home of the Hayden Haymakers sports teams, a nickname that needs some elaboration.

Hayden wasn't always Hayden. Until 1890 it was Hardenburg, a town that had grown up at a crossing of a Jennings County road and the railroad. The change came when

farmers began raising tons and tons of hay, which were shipped
from town on the Ohio and Mississippi (later the Baltimore and
Ohio) Railroad.

* * *

East of Hayden, a huge auto salvage yard is only partially
fenced from view of motorists. It will be one of many auto graveyards, scars on God's creation, we will see on this journey. Down
the road, cars are parked at the Home Restaurant, its diners
inside for mid-morning coffee.

U.S. 50 follows the railroad, once the B&O, now part of the
CSX System. Overhead, contrails from jet planes crisscross the
light blue sky on the eastern horizon, a contrast to the rails that
once carried passengers.

Small fields, woodlands, Christmas tree farms, body shops
and self storage units dot the roadside as the route turns from
east to northeast toward the city of North Vernon.

We are entering the Land of Winding Waters, a term for the
area drained by the Muscatatuck River. It is also a term used by
tourism groups to promote the natural scenic assets of Jennings
County.

Jennings County Middle School is off the road in a valley
near a new development. Across the highway is an old barn, huge
and in need of work. Barns in disrepair are now common sights
as towns push out to new corporate limits.

Ahead is Jennings County High School, a consolidation of
what were once small schools known as Brewersville, Butlerville,
Hayden, Lovett, Marion Township, North Vernon, Paris Crossing,
San Jacinto, Scipio, Vernon and Zenas.

Consolidation has been a mixed blessing. It has provided students with better opportunities for learning while robbing small
towns of the schools that had given them a sense of community.

* * *

We are in North Vernon, the road two-lane through the town
that once was crossed by three railroads. The days of the Iron
Horses are recalled at the city's Railroad Days held each summer,
the event centered around a depot that remains.

Off the road, a 1958 Chevrolet Bel-Air is for sale, a gem for any collector who wants to travel in mid-century style.

Like other cities, some businesses have departed North Vernon's old business district, moving north on Ind. 3, which crosses U.S. 50. A new library has followed the trend, leaving its old home abandoned.

Old buildings, many with two and three stories, are reminders of a North Vernon of an earlier time. Some have corona, decorative molded projections, at the top of the walls. It is a reflection of the time-consuming workmanship seldom seen in today's bland build-it-fast construction.

Some stores remain in the downtown area. One is a Christian book store, religious outlets now more prevalent than general book shops in small town.

Visitors, who stop at the book store, may frown at customers who enter and leave a nearby tattoo shop, this being an era when body decorations - if they be called decorations - are in vogue.

An old three-story brick with an 1899 date once was the home of the Masonic Lodge. Two doors away is Red Men Hall No. 99. The Red Men are gone but pigeons are warming in the sun on the east roof. The lower level is now a sports shop.

* * *

North Vernon, population 5,500, is by far the largest town in Jennings County, but the courthouse is to the south in the quiet, quaint town of Vernon, a short distance to the south on Ind. 3. It is a side trip worth taking for it is there history unfolds.

The 140-year-old courthouse remains, centered on a wooded square occupied by more row houses than businesses. Founded in 1815 on a bend of the Muscatatuck River by John Vawter, it is one of Indiana's oldest towns. Vawter's home was Gen. Lew Wallace's headquarters on his brief assignment to defend Vernon from Morgan's raiders during the Civil War.

A historical marker recalls Vernon's most eventful day: "Confederate Gen. John Hunt Morgan demanded the surrender of Vernon on July 11, 1863. When the defenders replied that Gen. Morgan must take it by hard fighting, he withdrew toward Dupont."

A scene on U.S. 50 in downtown North Vernon.

It was a calculated bluff that worked. Morgan had several thousand men. The volunteer and Union troops less than 1,000.

* * *

Back in North Vernon, U.S. 50 turns southeast as it heads out of town.

Off to the south is the Regal Rugs factory. Across the highways, we note an unusual block of homes. Six houses are side by side, almost identical, the stone exterior of each built with different kinds of rock - such as geodes from Indiana - inlaid in mortar joints.

Our questions about the houses are answered by Denise Shafer at the Jennings County Public Library. The houses, she tells us, were built around 1950 by Howard Couchman, who incorporated rock from each of what were then the 48 states. Couchman, who also was a fur dealer, had asked his delivery drivers to collect the rocks as they traversed the nation.

ville had its orgin when Quakers arrived in the 1850s
in covered wagons, bought land and built homes. One
settlers was John Morris, who became postmaster,
store and copied the name of the town from which he

g those settlers   was the Milhous family. Hannah
he mother of President Richard M. Nixon, was born on
r miles southeast of Butlerville, a place her grandpar-
ome in 1854. Hannah's parents moved in 1897 to Cali-
ere she later married Nixon's father.
of those pioneers   may have seen the arrival of the rail-
not the opening   of U.S. 50. That would come decades

e highway enters Butlerville from the west today it
umber company, a maker of pallets piled high on skids,
buyers who need them to stack merchandise to load
ks.
more churches, United Methodist and Baptist, are in
ndication the people of Butlerville are well pastored.
appears to have once been a general store at roadside is
d and for sale. Another old store in town is closed. The
l business left, it appears, is Lockridge Building Supply.
the railroad is an idle grain elevator, its days of service
s rusting into history. Like the town, it has seen better

aved on the front of a decaying building is "Butlerville
ool, 1904, J Murphy, trustee." The name has outlived
l. A belfry house   remains atop the front, but the bell is
ign is out front: 'Harvest Ministry Center, nondenomi-
Bible teaching. Worship 10 a.m. Sunday, Pastor Ron
ext to it is a two—story brick, its engraving etched with
lle School 1922.   J. E. Rine, Trustee." Like the other
s windows are broken, weeds have replaced grass and
s of former students are better left in the past than in
nt.
rville High School, which had been the home of the
basketball teams, closed in 1950 and students sent to
rnon, which later became a part of Jennings County

As an added touch to the houses
men to etch their names into stone
wood was used to make the fireplace m

Couchman was no ordinary build
napolis Star" in 1952 notes he preferre
ilies with children, explaining: "I like
couple should be prevented from ren
have children. After all, parents usua
keeping the rent paid and are more
renters."

Business sprawl follows the road o
is the Rock-A Billy sports bar and gril
another small factory and a housing de

Not far from town, U.S. 50 crosse
which flows southward as it is joined b
Creek.

* * *

A road sign tells us it is 73 miles t
trip to experience, not to speed past mil

A few miles northeast is a Rose Acr
storage facility for what is one of the na
ers. A Farm Bureau Co-op facility is ne
country.

A manufactured housing business i
in U.S. 50 that swings the road from r
away is a discount fabric outlet, which a
throughout southern Indiana.

A church, fittingly called Highway I
shelter on the grounds almost as big as t

Off to the north is the Muscatatuc
for Children. So is the Southeast Purdu
Center. Across the road is the Brush C
with an outdoor science laboratory.

A Mennonite Church occupies wha
building, a contrast to the antiques in a s

* * *

Butle
from Ohi
of those
opened a
had come

Amo
Milhous,
a farm fo
ents had
fornia, w

Man
road, bu
later.

As t
passes a
waiting
onto true

Two
town, an

Wha
abandon
Only reta

Nea
to farme
days.

Eng
High Sc
the scho
gone. A
national
Ford." N
"Butler
school,
memori
the pres

But
Bulldog
North

High School. The town's spirit may have departed with the students, its sense of community gone.

Across the street from the schools is an old two-story home, once the pride of its owner. It now is in disrepair and in need of attention and gallons of paint, like much of the town.

At the east edge of Butlerville a seat from a car is anchored on a deck near a pond, a relaxing spot from which to view the scenery or cast a fishing line.

The road continues to follow the railroad as it stretches to the east past small fields and woodlands.

* * *

Nebraska is another town whose past exceeds its present. Greyhounds traveling U.S. 50 no longer pick up passengers or stop at what was once a bus station. Trains no longer snatch mail pouches from their hooks where they were left by postmasters. The B&O Railroad depot is gone. So is a livery stable.

What is left is a part of the town platted by Robert Elliott in 1856, 11 years before Nebraska became a state. Nebraska, he claimed, came from an Osage Indian name for "flat water."

Boswell's Grocery remains open, though, as it has for decades, its two-story frame building dating back to 1908. But it, too, has changed. It no longer serves as the town post office. And it no longer sells shoes, clothing, hardware, whatever the general stores of the past once did. It is now a grocery and deli with sandwiches, lunch meat, pop, chips, ice cream . . . a convenience store for area residents and travelers.

Karen Boswell, who is at work at the store, suggests we talk with Junior Davidson, a town fixture for eight decades. We call his name outside the small camper behind the store where he lives, but he does not respond. A "Beware of Dog" sign keeps us away from the door.

There is little activity across U.S. 50 and the railroad tracks. Other than the store, the only retail outlet is a home with wood for sale. Otter Creek Baptist Church, circa 1848, still serves the purpose for which it was founded.

Nebraska may be rural, but it does have a health clinic at the east edge of town, not far from the Ripley County line.

RIPLEY COUNTY

A long trestle to the north off U.S. 50 carries the railroad tracks high over Little Long Branch, a creek that meanders to the southwest. The railroad will continue to parallel the road for miles.

A sawmill reflects the importance of timber to the southern Indiana economy.

It appears all is not happiness as we enter the county. A large sign, easily readable to passers by, complains, tersely: "Ripley County criminals welcome. The Ripley County prosecutor's office is a lazy, spineless piece of sh—." There is no further explanation, no credit claimed by the profane who posted it. Free speech sometimes comes at the expense of discretion.

* * *

Holton's western limits begin at a new cemetery, even though a cornfield separates it from the town a half-mile away.

Holton Liquors, a beer and wine outlet, is open. A homeowner, however, has found another way to get into the spirit of Christmas. His residence already is decorated for Christmas, which is more than two months away.

An old filling station, the kind with a roof over one bay, no longer sells gas. It is now operated by "Carf and Sons," a business open for on-road semi repair, light hauling and parts sales. "On call 24 hours a day," a sign notes.

Across U.S. 50 is what once was Holton High School, home of athletic teams called the Warhorses. The abandoned school, erected in 1956, is now for lease, the students gone since 1969. Area teen-agers now are the Raiders of South Ripley or the Eagles of Jac-Cen-Del at Osgood.

Disabled vehicles instead of school buses now occupy the parking lot. Like other Indiana towns, school closings cut away part of the heart of Holton where basketball once was the elixir for community spirit.

What looks to have been a restaurant in the business district is closed, the tables still in view through the windows. The Post Office is open, the Holton Town Hall is available to citizens, but there are few businesses and little activity in the old section of town.

That doesn't stop the town from sponsoring the annual Fly Wheelers Reunion, an exhibition of antique engines, arts, crafts and big servings of ham and beans.

Holton is another town that was moved out to the highway. A restaurant is open at the east edge, so is a busy Day-Nite food mart, a beer outlet, a radiator repair shop and a branch of the Napoleon State Branch.

Not far away, a woman is picking up debris from her lawn, items tossed out windows by undisciplined motorists.

We are entering tobacco country. East of Holton, a lumber yard offers for sale fire wood and tobacco sticks, which are used to cluster plants at harvest.

A Holton Water Company tank rises above the horizon not far from an antique mall. Golfers play the links at the Pine Hills golf course while a farmer spreads agricultural lime on his fields. An American flag flies at a suburban home ringed by a manicured lawn.

U.S. 421 joins U.S. 50 from the north, sharing the road into the heart of Versailles before it heads south toward Madison.

* * *

It is mid-morning in Versailles and McDonald's, the only fast food restaurant for miles, is packed. The place looks like it is a money machine. Its corner location is a prime spot at the intersection of the two U.S. highways, bringing in both travelers and area residents.

Inside, the place is crowded, the TV audio blending into the friendly chatter of 30 voices. The smoking section is packed for we are near an area where tobacco is a cash crop for farmers.

We choose a table away from the smoke, not far from a television set that is tuned to a Cincinnati station, its sound almost obscuring the voices of customers.

Two men, both retirees, are recalling their working years, interrupted at times by friends whose comments bring laugher. They are friendly, eager to talk about themselves and about Versailles. One is Gerald "Tug" Myers, the other Beverly - "my

Ripley County Courthouse in Versailles

parents must have been expecting a girl" - Shook. "Most people call me Shook," he explains.

"This is Versailles," one of them says, emphasizing "is" as he refers to McDonald's. "It's where most people meet. It's always busy, any time of day, because of the two roads. Each afternoon there are long traffic lines at the stoplight, especially northbound on U.S. 421."

They agree not a lot happens in Versailles, even though it is the county seat of Ripley County. "Oh, there are a couple of small factories here, like the metal plant (Ohio Rod Products which makes bicycle spokes and metal products). But some people have to drive 40 miles or so to Cincinnati to work," Shook says.

We bid farewell to "Tug" and "Shook," who wish us a safe trip.

Outside McDonald's a sign pleads for six new employees to work three-day weeks. Help in a good economy is hard to find, especially for restaurants as busy as McDonald's.

* * *

We drive a few blocks north of U.S. 50 to the older section of town. It is soon obvious Versailles could be called Tysonville for the name Tyson is big here. The nation has its Uncle Sam. Versailles had its "Uncle Jim."

He was Jim Tyson, a home town boy who left to make a fortune and, when he did, remembered the town fondly enough to become its benefactor.

Born in 1856, Jim Tyson walked out of school on April 3, 1871, into "The Gazette," a Versailles newspaper, and started to work. Fascinated by "tramp printers" who roamed from town to town, he worked in 20 or so towns and cities, seeing the nation and learning about life and the print business.

In 1890, he bought his own print shop in Chicago, where he met Charles Walgreen. The two men soon became friends and business partners, forming what would become the Walgreen Drug Company. Tyson became secretary-treasurer of the pharmaceutical chain, his wealth growing as the chain grew.

The Great Depression of the 1930s did not stop Tyson from sharing his fortune with Versailles. He announced in 1930 he would finance a new home for the Versailles Methodist Church.

Three months later the town became beneficiary of 18,000 shares of drug company capital stock, creating an endowment to be used "for the promotion of religious, educational, literary and social advancement of the Versailles community."

The results of the Tyson funds are obvious. The Tyson Temple Memorial Church is a town landmark, "Glory To God," noted on its front. An aluminum spire reaches 65 feet toward the heavens.

A critic once called the temple "a conglomeration of the Tyson impression of the Taj Mahal, ancient Egyptian arcade and world-famous places and cathedrals." Those were places Tyson likely saw on his frequent trips around the world.

Tyson money also financed a new school in 1938, a building said to embody "the most modern features known to school construction." The school was used until South Ripley High School opened in 1966, consolidating Versailles, Cross Plains, Holton and New Marion. It now is the Tyson Auditorium and the Versailles Community Center, its purpose to serve all of Ripley County. It still is the scene of area high school basketball games.

Near the church on Tyson Street is the Tyson Library, built and endowed with revenue from the trust. "The money still pays our salaries," an employee of the library explains.

All the Tyson buildings have incorporated identical features, the front exteriors of pale yellow ceramic brick.

Not far away is the 140-year-old Ripley County Courthouse. It is in excellent condition after extensive remodeling in the mid-1990s which saw the whitewash removed and the bricks restored to their original color. The clock on the tower is keeping perfect time, the chimes of 10 o'clock reverberating through the town.

A marker on the east side of the square notes the town's flirtation with history: "Morgan's Raid - July 8-13, 1863. Gen. John Hunt Morgan, confederate cavalry commander, occupied Versailles on Sunday afternoon, July 12. Having seized the county treasury he moved north at 4 p.m. as Union forces began to close in upon him."

A granite memorial - "God, Duty, Honor, Country" - pays tribute to Ripley County veterans of all wars from the Revolutionary to Somalia. Scenes of ground and naval action is depicted on the huge granite slabs. Bricks, engraved with names of men and women who served their country, are around the memorial.

On an opposite corner, a marker recalls that a Masonic Hall occupied part of the square with the courthouse from 1847 to 1918. The sign notes that some of Morgan's raiders took jewels from the lodge officers on his 1863 excursion. Gen. Morgan, a free mason himself, ordered them returned.

Like other counties, government bureaucracy has outgrown the original courthouse and some Ripley County offices now share space in a building across the street to the north.

On a corner of the square is the Spencer-Tyson Drug Store. The Ripley County Historical Society is in an old bank building. The Courthouse Inn, Bar and Grill and Beer Garden is on the southeast corner of the square as it has been since 1865. If walls could talk those in the restaurant likely could reveal a million stories about the town and visiting lawyers who came to Versailles to plead cases in the courthouse across the street.

The town boasts of the annual Versailles Pumpkin Show, held the last weekend of September as it has been for 95 years. On most other weekends, Versailles is peaceful and quiet, a good place to linger for motorists in no hurry to return to the highway.

* * *

At the east edge of Versailles, U.S. 50 makes a sharp decline toward Laughery Creek, which slices through Versailles State Park. The park is a place to relax, fish or operate paddle boats on a 230-acre lake, walk the wooded hills or return in July for the annual fireworks.

A sharp curve leads U.S. 50 through a valley before the road rises and a passing lane allows slower cars to pull to the right. Up ahead, Ind. 129 leads north to the town of Delaware.

* * *

Elrod is a community whose length exceeds its width. Houses and farms front U.S. 50 for 1.8 miles between its town limit signs. A small concrete block structure painted blue is identified as the Washington Township Community Building. Not far away the Washington Baptist Church warns, "Death will be gained only if the price is your reason to live."

A garage along the road is closed. The only retail business we note is a farm which offers pumpkins for sale.

* * *

East of Elrod, U.S. 50 becomes a four-lane road near the intersection of Ind. 101.

DEARBORN COUNTY

Near the entrance to Dearborn County, an old motel no longer is in business, motorists now preferring to spend their nights in chain motels near restaurants in urban settings. What looks to have been a truck stop is abandoned. A blue tarpaulin covers items outdoors at an antique business, which when open has beanie babies for sale.

Beef cattle graze in pastures off to the north of the highway. Another small motel now appears to be occupied by more permanent residents.

* * *

A sign greets visitors: "Welcome to Dillsboro, A good place to live. Founded in 1830." Mathias Whetstone laid out the town and named it for Gen. James Dills, a soldier in the War of 1812 who included Gen. William Henry Harrison among his friends. What was first Dillsborough later was shortened to Dillsboro.

U.S. 50, which once passed through the heart of the town, now runs along the north side. Dillsboro is small, but self-sufficient with stores, businesses, banks, a retirement center and service stations.

The downtown area looks unchanged over the years. Unlike other towns, Dillsboro appears to have kept most of its businesses in the old downtown district. The drug store is an example. It looks much as it would have a half-century ago, except the soda fountain is gone. A lone pharmacist accepts and fills prescriptions, unlike the stable of druggists at giant drug outlets.

Dillsboro no longer has a high school, its athletes once known as Bulldogs are now the Knights of South Dearborn, a few miles away.

There still is pride in its citizens, however. They tell visitors Dillsboro is a town that offers rural living with access to the services of metropolitan areas, a combination that allows it to attract and retain businesses.

* * *

East of Dillsboro, rolling farm land lines the road. A Farm Bureau Co-op elevator is open and a Mack Truck sales business is in what looks like a giant round barn.

The road is on a ridge, the panorama to the east a spectacular sight. Hills and valleys are in view as the terrain drops toward the Ohio River Valley at Aurora.

An Aurora water tower, painted red and white, colors of the South Dearborn Knights, towers over the hills. The school can be seen in the distance to the north. Off the road is the Aurora Casket Company.

U.S. 50 drops sharply toward the river, a sign warning motorist to watch for falling rock from the outcroppings which jut from the cliffs formed by the road cuts.

* * *

A view of the Ohio from high over Aurora

Aurora is a river town, much of its history written on the turbulent waters of the mighty Ohio which bends south at this point. The commerce of the city of 4,000 is tied to the river, reflected in the names of two downtown streets, one called Importing, one Exporting.

Its most famous landmark is Hillforest Mansion, which overlooks the Ohio. The Italian Renaissance home is symmetrical with broad overhangs, ornately carved brackets, arched windows, balconies and porches. Rounded collonades topped by a "pilot house" belvedere give it a steamboat like appearance.

On this visit, Hillforest, which is on the National Register of Historic places, is under repair, too historic to fall into disrepair. It was the home for the last half of the 19th century to Thomas Gaff, an industrialist and financier.

High above the river is Veraestau, a pioneer home of note that now looks as if it could be a plantation mansion. Its 425 foot elevation provides an awesome view of the river valley, Aurora below and Lawrenceburg upstream. Veraestau is now operated by the Historic Landmarks Foundation, which conducts tours by appointment only.

The home is on Glenmary Lane. A private paved entrance lined by giant oaks leads to the home on the bluff.

No appointment, however, is needed for another imposing view of the Ohio Valley. We take Langley Heights Street up a steep incline to York Avenue. The peak provides a wide angle view of Aurora, a vista overlooking three states, Indiana to the north, Ohio to the northeast and Kentucky to the east.

Back in downtown Aurora, we note an art shop, appropriately named Aurora Borealis.

The city is considered a part of the Greater Cincinnati metroplex, an urban area. But Aurora has reminders of its rural past. An old-time grain elevator - Aylor and Meyer Incorporated - features Romeo corn products, Romeo flour, Rainbow feed, roofing, fencing, salt, fertilizer and an elevator. "The feeder's silent partner," a sign adds.

The old building is a reminder of the past for a farm boy of the 1930s who remembers taking wheat to a similar mill to be ground into flour.

A railroad depot remains nearby, but the days of passenger service has long passed. It is now for sale, a challenge for preservationists who may want to save it as a part of Aurora's history.

Restaurants recommended by residents include the Wild Duck Cafe, open on a paddlewheel boat anchored at river's edge from May to October; Applewood by the River and Steamboat Clinton, another fitting name for a river town.

* * *

U.S. follows the river upstream toward Lawrenceburg, the roadsides lined with restaurants, convenience stores and assorted businesses. Traffic is heavy and left turns keep motorists alert, unlike the casual drive in open areas to the west.

A huge new Wal-Mart Supercenter, which includes a McDonald's and a grocery, is open. It is full-service shopping, which may further erode the customer base of small independent businesses. Apartment units are being built into the hills away from the road and the river. A Skyline Chili outlet is on the left, an indication we are approaching Cincinnati and its renowned chili parlors.

* * *

Lawrenceburg is sometimes called "Whiskey City" and for good cause. Distilleries have played a part in its history for almost 150 years. A sign on a huge plant off the road proclaims, "Seagram's Distilleries - since 1857." Another notes "Lawrenceburg - Home of Seagram - Spirit of Quality."

The Joseph Seagram's & Sons distilleries are called the largest of their kind in the nation and a source of employment and fame for Lawrenceburg, one of Indiana's oldest town in the third oldest county in the state. Both the town and Dearborn County were formed in 1803 and Lawrenceburg soon became a path for settlers heading north and west.

It's not surprising that one of the city's most popular restaurants is Whisky's, a family dining spot noted for ribs, steaks and seafood. It is in a union of two historic buildings, both dating back beyond 1850. The menu is extensive, the food is good and the luncheon prices reasonable.

Lawrenceburg's historic district is between U.S. 50 and the river, protected by a levee built after the 1937 Ohio River flood devastated both the city and Aurora. Streets are wide, homes are big and well-maintained, but some old commercial buildings are unused and awaiting attention.

Mansion type homes, some dating back to the start of the 19th Century, can be found near the levee. The Dearborn County Courthouse, fronted by four columns, was built in 1871 and reflects the attention given to its preservation.

On Walnut Street, the spire at the St. Lawrence Catholic Church towers over the city. Still open down the street in a residential area is the Walnut Theater, its marquee noting it is showing "Practical Magic." It is a rarity for most neighborhood theaters have disappeared, replaced by eight-to-sixteen screen operations in suburban locations.

Lawrenceburg High School is off the road away from the river as it has been for more than 50 years. Aurora and Lawrenceburg had one of Indiana's most intense sports rivalries until Aurora became part of the South Dearborn consolidation.

A sign at the edge of U.S. 50 boasts that Lawrenceburg is home to the world's largest riverboat casino. The boast is short-lived. A week later, a larger one opened down river near New Albany across from Louisville, Ky. No matter! This riverboat is elaborate, an environment conducive to raising state revenues while taking money from participants at slot machines and games of chance.

Off U.S. 50 is a Holiday Inn Express and a parking lot for gamblers who want to be shuttled to and from the riverboat, allowing them to count their money en route and their wins or losses on the way back.

A road sign tells us it is 24 miles to downtown Cincinnati.

* * *

Off to the northeast of U.S. 50 is Greendale, squeezed between Lawrenceburg and the Ohio border in the rolling hills northwest of the river. Annexation in 1997 doubled the size of the city, whose limits extend to Ohio and include the bottomlands. The I-75 and U.S. 50 interchange, which links the tri-state area of Indiana, Kentucky and Ohio, appears ready for development. Unlike U.S. 50 through Lawrenceburg there are few businesses along the route as it nears Ohio.

The Buckeye State is ahead.

CHAPTER 2

OHIO

HAMILTON COUNTY

Travel allows us to be who we are at the moment. Those we meet on the road do not judge us for what we have been. They do not evaluate our character, mentally tally our assets and liabilities or rate us on a scale of accomplishments. To them, we have no past, no future. We are what they see today without the blemishes of the past or the successes of tomorrow.

* * *

We have entered Ohio, crossing a straight north-south border that separates the state from Indiana. The Ohio River at this point is three or so miles to the south.

U.S. 50 remains four lanes, but the pavement is narrower and rougher, a seemingly no-man's area, a forgotten highway far from the attention of lawmakers up in Columbus.

The roadside is a mixture of small farm fields, scrub land and houses. An old corn crib is a reminder of decades ago when farmers drove their wagons into an opening in the center, then scooped corn into bins on each side. It is far different than the steel grain bins corn is stored in at most farms today.

We pass through Elizabethtown, a small community where elementary students are at play on the grounds, delighted to be free of the classroom if only briefly.

Not far away a Sunoco station advertises for a part time meat cutter, an unlikely combination of gasoline and pork.

Beyond is a giant junk yard, or to be politically correct, a recyclable center and landfill. It can expect to do more recycling, now that more and more Americans are accepting the trend to convert packaging materials to new uses.

We enter another desolate area, the landscape somewhat unsightly near the Whitewater River. We note the railroad now runs to the south between U.S. 50 and the Ohio River, which is just a short distance away.

* * *

We enter a small town built into the hills north of the Ohio and are greeted with: "Welcome to the Village of Cleves - Founded in 1818." The population, we learn later, is 2,300.

It is good to see the old depot still in use, not abandoned like some in other towns on what was the B&O. This one at Cleves is now, a sign reveals, "The Dental Depot." It appears to be a good use for an old building, a practical way to save a landmark.

* * *

Cleves is an old town, but not as old as North Bend, its neighbor to the south. North Bend was born as a river town in 1789, its history anchored on the hills above. Its narrow streets still run up and around the hills past old homes that date back a century or more.

North Bend never grew much - its population now listed as 541, but its place in American history is much bigger. A sign off U.S. 50 notes the tomb of President William Henry Harrison. His grandson, Benjamin Harrison, who also grew up to be president, was born on a farm not far from the Ohio near North Bend.

Up on one of the hills is Taylor High School, home of the Yellow Jackets. It is, appropriately, located on Harrison Avenue, a daily reminder to students of the towns role in America's history.

* * *

At North Bend, U.S. 50 turns from south to southeast and follows the river to the town of Addyston, population 1,200. Tasteful signs that line U.S. 50 tell us Addyston is an "architecturally unique village on the national register of historic places." Its homes are planted firmly into the terrain as it rises over the river.

U.S. 50, now a four-lane road through Addyston, once was a narrow two-lane route a block or so to the north through the business area. Old buildings with outside steel fire escapes line the narrow streets which wind into the hills, some on banks above a small stream that flows toward the Ohio. The town post office is in a small building painted dark red.

* * *

From the corner of our eye we detect some old gasoline pumps, the kind used decades ago before the 12-bay stations of today.

Fascinated, we circle a block and return to what a sign tells us is "Buzz's Museum." Working out front on an old riding mower is Buzz Bowman, owner, operator and a collector extraordinaire.

Buzz Bowman at his museum in Addyston

Don't ask him "What's new?" He is more likely to respond to "What's old?"

Buzz is not your average antique buff. He's a master at his hobby. "I'm collecting these now," he says as he nods toward the Wheel Horse he is repairing. "Let me show you around," he says, showing he is as adept at hospitality as he is at collecting.

In front of his museum are just some of the 71 gasoline pumps he has collected, the oldest a 1912 model. Most are the kind with handles which pumped the fuel up into glass cylinders from where gravity let it flow into gasoline tanks of trucks and cars.

He shows us some of the pumps, probably would all 71 if we had the time. But there are other items to see, thousands of them, and Buzz is eager to show us them, too.

We nod when he asks, "You like old stuff?" Our response is enough. He leads us through the museum, where he explains, "I have anything here you would want to see." It is not an exaggeration.

You name it, Buzz has it: Fishing lures, 750 or more, cans of oil, never opened, from around the world. One is from Iraq, with Iraqi printing on the side, another from the United Kingdom. Others are from almost every country where oil is refined.

There are license plates from every state and every nation that has cars that need tags. A sign with a picture of a policeman that once stood in the street to slow traffic is among the collection. So are antiques and hundreds of small toys and thousands of other items, each in numerous numbers. The museum is full of items collectors crave. If a manufacture made it, chances are Buzz probably has it.

"I've got some benches out of that old park," he says, referring to Crosley Field where the baseball Reds once played.

"Home is right here," he says, taking us inside where more items are stored. An old beauty shop has been recreated, a tribute to his wife who was once a beautician.

"Buzz's Museum" didn't happen by chance. It is an accumulation of 32 years of search, research, hard work, a lot of travel and a desire to put his retirement years to good use. Let him explain:

"Well, I quit smoking. I quit drinking. I quit gambling. I quit hunting. I quit fishing. When I quit working (he made skids for 30 years), I said to myself I had to find something to do."

Distance, he says, is not a factor if there is a collectible to be found. "I go as far north, south, east or west as the road goes," he says. And his quest extends throughout the earth, as far as mail is delivered and from wherever items are shipped.

It is a hobby that has brought the world to him. "Lord yes," he says, "people stop by . . . from all over the world. Germany,

France, Japan, from wherever tourist come. They see the museum from down on U.S. 50, especially when the leaves are off the trees, and they find us like you did."

Visitors are warned, however. Do not - repeat do not - expect to buy anything - repeat anything - from Buzz Bowman. Nothing is for sale. His joy comes from finding and keeping items. Not in selling them.

But he might buy an item brought to the museum. "We buy anything old," his business card says.

It is obvious Bowman has found something to do other than smoke, gamble, fish and hunt. And, for him, it seems more enjoyable than any of those things.

* * *

Embedded in the sidewalk in front of "Buzz's Museum" is a marker noting a point the Ohio River reached during the 1937 flood. The road continues to run southeast as it follows a bend in the river toward downtown Cincinnati, 15 miles away.

Near Sayler Park, a McDonald's is located in a super station/convenience store. It is the first fast food outlet we have seen

since Lawrenceburg.

Not far away is the Cincinnati city limit sign. The Ohio River is a long football pass away from U.S. 50, which continues its circular path of least resistance into the heart of the city.

* * *

In Cincinnati, U.S. 50 no longer is a quiet road through farms and small towns. It is a part of the traffic and transportation system of a metropolis, where space is a premium and business is its heartbeat.

U.S. 50 eases through downtown Cincinnati, its downtown a basin ringed with hills. "Queen City," its admirers boast. "The most beautiful of America's inland cities," Winston Churchill called it.

No matter! It is not a city to see by cars. Motorists on U.S. 50 need to park off the road to better see the downtown on foot.

Platted in 1788, Cincinnati was opened for settlement a few years later after the defeat of the Ohio Indians at Fallen Timbers. Riverboats began arriving, via the Mississippi and Ohio Rivers, in the early 1800s.

It is now home to businesses, industries, corporations, museums, universities, a zoo, and sports franchises like the Reds and the Bengals, which play home games on the waterfront between the river and U.S. 50. The big radio topic on this day is whether to build a new baseball stadium next to existing Cinergy Field or locate it elsewhere.

Almost lost in the maze of Interstates 74, 75 and 71 as they converge from the north toward the river is U.S. 50, its signs at times hard to detect amid the traffic.

It is the Interstates that bring workers from Indiana and Kentucky as well as the city's suburbs to jobs in downtown Cincinnati. It is the city that is the economic - and social and entertainment - center of the tri-state area.

U.S. 50 accompanies six-lane Interstate 71 for a short distance before it resumes its individual two-lane path around a bend in the Ohio. High rise apartment buildings dominate the hills to the north, a concrete retaining wall reaching around a curve.

To the east, U.S. 50 passes through some undeveloped areas just a few miles from downtown Cincinnati, a buffer of sorts between the city and the suburbs beyond.

* * *

The road again becomes four-lane as it approaches the Village of Mariemont, a hidden jewel tucked into the hem of Cincinnati. In distance, Mariemont is 10 miles from downtown, but light years away from its noise and traffic.

Strict zoning has kept housing areas for houses, business areas for business, creating what looks like the planned community it was designed to be in the 1930s. Streets are tree lined, some divided by manicured islands. Businesses are restricted to districts called "Old Town" and "Village Square."

Many of the homes are architecturally designed, each different from the next for this is not a one-size-fits-all community. An Architectural Review Board is charged with maintaining a high standard of community development.

It appears to have met its responsibility to the village's 3,200 residents.

* * *

U.S. 50 again becomes two-lane past Mariemont near Plainville, where it turns to the northeast, passes a wooded area and becomes four lane into Terrace Park, population 2,200.

CLERMONT COUNTY

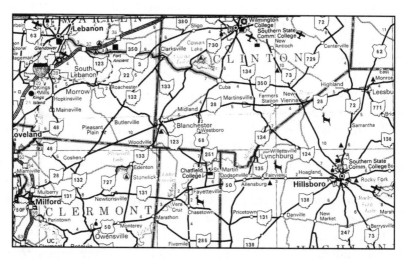

Milford, its population of 5,700 living in an older community, is a short distance away. One of many suburbs of Cincinnati, it has its own stores and businesses. It appears to be unchanged, unlike some other suburbs that have lost their personalities in an attempt to keep pace with progress.

Traffic on a section of U.S. 50 through Milford is maintained by old, somewhat difficult to see, stoplights that dangle from wires that stretch across the pavement. The road does not appear to have been improved for years, which may be a blessing for those residents who prefer to be away from traffic. A wider road

could lead to population growth which would add to the congestion.

* * *

A short distance from Milford, U.S. 50 crosses under Interstate 275 which circles Cincinnati, its route entering Kentucky to
the south before sneaking past a corner of Indiana near Greendale.

Greater Cincinnati is behind us. U.S. 50 heads south over a
winding, two-lane course with few opportunities for hurried
motorists to pass. It makes no difference to us for we have no
timetable, no deadline, no schedule to meet.

The road follows the East Fork of the Little Miami River into
Perrintown, a wide spot along the road where activity appears
centered at a convenience store. Buildings sit close to traffic lanes
without sidewalks to divide them.

The road continues to follow the Little Miami for a short distance before turning east. A Mail Pouch Tobacco sign covers part
of a barn and round bales of hay dot a field as we enter farm
country. A sign points to Red Fox Stables for city dwellers who
own or are interested in horses.

To the east, the road winds its way to the top of a hill, then
passes a log cabin. A silo stands forlorn, its barn gone with the
past. A few farms line the road as do small subdivisions, home to
commuters who have jobs back in the city.

Not far away, in contrast, is an ancient brick home, painted
white, as much a part of the past as the highway itself.

There is little traffic, those who prefer faster travel having
taken four-lane Ohio 32, which is less than four miles to the
South.

We are nearing Owensville when we pass Pattison Park, a
40-acre site given to the Clermont County Park District by
Aletheia Pattison, daughter of John M. Pattison, Ohio's 43rd governor. The park has two short trails and picnic and recreational
facilities, plus an outdoor gezebo and rustic lodge.

* * *

At Owensville, a sign informs us the town of 1,050 was the
birthplace of former Gov. Pattison.

A huge convenience store with a number of gas bays is at roadside, a far different place than the mom and pop gasoline stations with two pumps where motorists once stopped.

An independent hardware store remains open, the town too small to attract a giant retailer seeking to eliminate smaller competitors. Others stores are along the highway, built close to the pavement like the houses, mostly two-story I-frame structures that are reminders of the past.

Not far from a new apartment development is a two-story home of native stone, its wooden windows making it appear unchanged over the years. Not far away on a hill is another old house, shutters at its windows.

A sports complex and the impressive Northeastern High School is at the east edge of town.

* * *

The historic Hartman Log Cabin, another Clermont County park facility, is four miles east of Owensville. A herb and vegetable garden and an orchard are on the five acres that surround the restored 1800s cabin. A gravel trail leads to a pioneer cemetery, the history of the area written on grave markers.

U.S. 50 takes a straighter line as it heads east through farm country on its way to Marathon. A sign promotes the Seven Caves, an attraction 40 miles ahead. A housing development is being built here in the open spaces 20 miles from the east leg of I-275 which rings metropolitan Cincinnati.

* * *

We enter Marathon, a small community with houses near the road, unchanged, much as the road has remained. The town has a grocery, a post office in an old house and a tavern named "Just One More."

Farms begin at the east edge of Marathon. Christmas trees grow on one, a grape vineyard on another.

Up ahead is Monterey, a wide spot in the road with a market. A church has a sign welcoming a new minister. A message on a bulletin board at another church asks: "Where Do you Want to Spend Eternity? Smoking or Non-Smoking?"

The traffic lanes on U.S. 50 are wider than back to the west, but the road remains two lane. There are few businesses along the route.

BROWN COUNTY

Reuben Keeton amid his walking canes

It is the unexpected encounters that make traveling more than casual drives between two points. Reuben Keeton provided one of those pleasures.

We find him on a rise off to the north of U.S. 50 west of Fayetteville at his window on the world. Keeton is at work making canes and walking sticks, his work on display for passing motorists.

"That's Keeton with two e's," he jokes. "You don't get to put an 'a' in the name until you're wealthy." He greet us with Saturday night on-the-town friendliness, making conversation easy.

Keeton is wearing a blue Ford cap, his blue and white shirt covered in front with a knee-length apron. His work tools are in the back of a pickup with a camper shell parked under a grove of trees. His trailer home is back further from the road, surrounded by the 17 acres he owns.

"Been making these since 1987 when I retired from Celotex - worked there from '46 to '87, making roofing. I couldn't count how many canes and walking sticks I've made."

There are dozens available for buyers who may stop. He shows off some of the better ones, some from special wood, others from native trees.

"I have some made of sourwood, which doesn't grow around here. It stinks when cut, sour like, so I guess that's where it got its name. The others are made from sumac, sassafras, hickory, beech and other kinds of wood.

"You have to cut the wood in the fall when the sap is down," he adds.

Each cane carries his initials with abbreviations for the type wood, "ch" for cherry for example, and the year noted by the last two digits, such as "98."

Prices range from $5 to $500. The most expensive, hickory, part of its bark peeled, the wood rubbed and finished with 12 to 15 coats of linseed oil. Some of the bark remains to give the stick the look of a rattlesnake, beads used to indicate eyes.

No matter the number of sales, Keeton is content with what he does. "I had never done much woodworking until I retired from a job that demanded production, production, production. You need to take your time to do something right. Do that and it will sell. When I started doing this I said I would not hurry, that I would take my time. And that's what I do.

"I don't sell a lot of them, but I'm satisfied. We have them for sale here in warm months and in Florida (North Petersburg), where we spend the winters. Sold 100 down there in the winter of 1997-98," he explains.

Keeton sometimes takes time off to fish and hunt. "I love to hunt with both bow and muzzle loader. My nephew keeps telling me I only get one shot that way. I say, 'that's all I want.'" And chances are all he needs.

We depart with a Reuben Keeton walking stick, envious of a man who likes what he does and does what he likes.

* * *

Up ahead is the unincorporated community of Vera Cruz, its caution light and scattered houses making it too small to be listed as an Ohio village.

Bell tower atop Fayetteville Fire Station

Fayetteville is near the northern tip of a narrow panhandle of Brown County that extends to the north. It's an old town, incorporated in 1818. Buildings of that era extend almost to the roadway, housing a market, gift shop and a saddle and tack shop for equestrians.

The road through the town of 400 residents is fronted by dwellings, including row houses with steps, unchanged by time.

A tavern called "By Crackery" is at the side of the highway in a building old enough to have provided libation to residents and visitors for a century.

The two-story Fayetteville Fire Department and Rescue Station is in an old two-story brick with a bell tower at the top, a device once used to call firemen to action. Across the street is a barber shop in a building 12 by 18 feet.

A small building fronting on U.S. 50 houses offices for the town mayor, police department, village council and board of public affairs.

Fayetteville is the center for the Southwestern Bookmobile Center, which makes regular stops at 16 sites in Brown County. It is an information resource for area residents who do not have direct access to libraries.

If the world has passed by on U.S. 50, no one in town seems to mind.

We are 20 miles from the city of Hillsboro. Beyond Fayetteville the road continues to the north, somewhat straighter but still narrow. A tractor, a wide planter behind it, makes passing difficult, but this is farm country and there is no reason to rush.

Those who travel U.S. 50 soon learn it is not the quickest distance between two points.

HIGHLAND COUNTY

Some old I-frame homes along one side of the road are in contrast to newer ranch style homes on the other. The soil looks marginal but the fields are large. A few old barns - which slowly are disappearing from rural America- remain along the road.

A service station/convenience store is at the edge of Dodsonville, a community that is yet to find its way onto road maps. Dodsonville is a caution light, a grain elevator that appears to be out of business and a park area at the edge of town.

Ahead is a nice house with manicured lawn, its flag waving in the warm afternoon breeze. Not far away is an abandoned farmstead, its home and barn fallen into the abyss of history.

* * *

Allensburg is small, too. Its population too few to be recorded. A Shell station is open, but an old motel, its business gone with the lure of fancier chains with advertising dollars, is no longer open to tourists. Like others, it likely saw its business decline when four-lane interstates without stoplights linked cities.

The road is narrow with few places to pass. Just outside Allensburg, we are caught behind a painter, ladders strapped atop his van. We are 300 yards behind when, in slow motion it seems, one of the ladders begins to slide from the van. It glides onto the pavement, then slides along our path. We ease into the oncoming lane to avoid the hazard. The painter slows his van, pulls off at a side road and waves, grateful there has been no damage as we pass. His ladders, we are sure, will be more secure when he returns to the road.

* * *

The road runs straight east from Allensburg into Fairview, the speed limit dropping from 55 to 45 mph. Fairview is another small town that may soon become larger, a sign revealing a new subdivision is "coming soon."

Prime building sites are available, "prices reduced," but no houses have been started.

A trucking terminal is west of Hillsboro. A nearby auto parts store appears to be busy. Not far away is a used car lot. It will be the first of hundreds we will see on the road toward Washington for cars are among the prize possessions of almost every American and buying and trading them is an industry in itself.

A salvage yard is nearby, a depository for discarded cars no longer cherished.

* * *

At the edge of Hoagland - a town too small for even a caution light - an old Oliver farm tractor is for sale. A Tasty Freeze is open but there are few other businesses.

As we near Hillsboro, we pass another auto sales lot, a lumber yard, a manufactured housing outlet, a farm implement business, self storage units and still a second used car sales lot. It is obvious Hillsboro is a trading center for this section of Ohio.

* * *

U.S. 50 winds into town over rolling terrain past a Dairy Queen, an office complex and a motel. The impressive Hillsboro High School is on a knoll at the west edge of town.

We have entered the city of Hillsboro, a community of pride, the seat of Highland County government, the home of Elisa Jane Thompson, a leader in the temperance union.

We stop at Magee's Snack Shop on the side of U.S. 50 near the Highland County Courthouse Square. It is 2 p.m. on a Saturday afternoon and each table in the long, narrow cafe is filled as are stools at the counter. It is a down home diner, a place where a grill is in view and most customers know each other.

A brochure at the restaurant promotes the Festival of the Bells, an annual July 4th event big enough to cause U.S. 50 traffic to be detoured through the heart of town. The event, a waitress tells us, stems from the days when a bell factory was a Hillsboro industry. A different bell - each edition limited - is fashioned each year for the festival that has become one of the city's major events.

The Bells Opera House remains a downtown fixture, a marker noting its historic significance.

An old theater - The Colony - is on the courthouse square, a place where movies sometimes are still shown. Once the Festival of the Bells opens it will feature Toddy Henry and the Hee Haw Opry Style - "high energy, outrageously funny and fast paced," a brochure promises.

Another major event each year in the city of 6,500 is Hillsboro Flag Day USA, observed each June 14 at Liberty Park in town.

The two-story brick courthouse, its columns and dome imposing enough to be on a post card, is the oldest still in use in Ohio. The sheriff's office remains in a building connected to the Courthouse. A memorial to veterans of all wars is on the lawn, which is the site each summer Saturday of a farmers' market.

Down Main Street, which also is U.S. 50, is the Parker House, once an elegant hotel. Its second floor ballroom still holds memories of a more formal time in American history, a time when big bands played music in small towns and residents dressed in their finest suits and gowns.

Several attempts to open businesses in the building have been unsuccessful. It now is a ghost of the past, when visitors spent nights in downtown hotels instead of passing through in search of an overnight stop where one motel looks much like another.

Unlike some county seats, most store fronts in Hillsboro are occupied, not vacant.

Near the Courthouse is the Highland House Museum, a 1840s classic Federal Style building, which once was a home, a hotel and a restaurant. On the National Register of Historic Places, it houses the Highland County Historical Society as well as an extensive collection of memorabilia from the area's past.

It is not easy to leave Hillsboro. It is as American as apple pie, a town whose history predates the highway, a place where buildings are old, but enthusiasm is young, a city worth a longer visit.

* * *

We enter Southern Ohio's hill country east of Hillsboro. A vista extends across the miles, opening a panorama of trees, hills and pastures that portray the beauty of this section of the state. Grass lands and hay fields are interwoven among the corn and soybeans.

The road twists and turns again, rolling as the land undulates.

We enter the town of Boston, where the only business activity on this day appears to be at a yard sale and at an office for manufactured homes.

Abandoned is an old filling station, the kind where motorists pulled under a roofed extension and ordered gasoline from an attendant who volunteered to check the oil and clean the bugs from the windshield.

A Methodist Church is off the highway, but there is little else in Boston.

U.S. 50 continues to snake its way eastward, opening a broad view toward the hills beyond.

An old motel now appears to be used as apartments. A flea market is at roadside but the traffic is light and customers few. A rural restaurant has a few late afternoon diners.

An old I-frame pioneer house, made of brick, has been expanded, its additions in frame rather than masonry.

A short distance south of U.S. 50 is Rocky Fork State Park, its 2,080-acre lake a major attraction. Two swimming beaches and 200 campsites are in the park. Fishing, boating, camping, hunting, hiking, fishing and picnicking are permitted.

* * *

We arrive in Rainsboro, a hamlet at roadside, its buildings almost within outstretched arms of the cars that pass.

Dave Frye greets us at Ye Olde Village Antiques, the building decorated with flags and filled with collectibles in search of buyers. The building, explains Frye, who operates the store with his wife, Lori, is part of the history of Rainsboro and of U.S. 50.

Frye is friendly, applies no pressure to make a sale. He is more eager to give us an overview of the town. The building, he says, was a church before it was moved from a block west to its corner location. It also was used to store horse collars,

Dave Frye at antique shop at side of U.S. 50

implements and other agricultural items. If its walls could talk, they would reveal sermons long forgotten, negotiations between sellers and buyers, from times past.

The brick structure across the street, once a store as well as the town post office, is vacant. But that may change. It is owned by Frye's landlord, Ray Chaney, who plans to restore it to its original appearance. It's a project that will take a year, maybe two or more, but one that will retain a segment of Rainsboro's history.

Frye shows us a picture of the Rainsboro of the past. It dates back to a time when a walkway stretched from one building to the other across what was then the dirt road that would become U.S. 50. The road appears no wider now than it was then. But its surface is paved and cars have replaced buggies and horseless carriages.

There are other old buildings, most of which are brick, one which once was a school.

Frye, whose grandfather once carried mail with a horse and buggy, seems to know Rainsboro's past. "Believe it or not," he reveals, "the town had a lot of wealth back when it was on a freight route for teamsters. They would come from Chillicothe to Bainbridge and stay overnight, then come from Bainbridge to Rainsboro and stop again for the night, a day's travel covering just 12 to 15 miles.

"A big hotel was here, so were a livery stable and three or four stores. A horse race track was a half-mile south. It was a boom town."

Those boom days are gone. Rainsboro, however, is showing signs of rebirth. Nearby lakes are attracting visitors. A tire store, a "certified" child care center, and other businesses are in town or nearby.

Frye has not been disappointed over his move to Rainsboro from Greenfield. "So far we're happy with this location," he says of his business. "People have treated us well."

And chances he has returned the kindness they've shown.

* * *

We will soon learn that U.S. 50 in this area of Ohio could be called Antique Alley.

As we leave Rainsboro rows of hills rise in the distance. It is a spectacular view for there are no semitrailers to block the view. Farms with rolling hills and lush grass are ideal for the dairy herds and beef cattle that graze on them.

Traffic is heavier as we near the Seven Caves - a national landmark - and the Paint Creek State Park. My traveling companion is no spelunker, doesn't like caverns, so we choose to visit the park instead. A two-mile drive leads to the a dam, high above the beach and the water below. A bridge over a deep canyon offers another excellent view of a creation of nature.

The park in mid-summer of 1998 was the site of the Kenda Knite Glo 12-hour ultra endurance mountain race for mountain bikers or anyone else looking for an adventure.

* * *

Back on the road a rest area is a welcome - and unusual sight - on a non-interstate route.

ROSS COUNTY

Not far away is a small private airport, a few small airplanes in the hangars. A silo stands alone, its barn gone. An old brick farm house is on a knoll that overlooks fields nestled in the lowland. We are in a valley between the hills with little debris along the road except for trash that awaits a scavenger service.

A sign warning motorists to be alert for horses and buggies indicates we are in Amish country.

* * *

Bainbridge, population 975, boasts that it is the home of the nation's first dental school. A museum at the west entrance to town validates the claim.

An old two-story sandstone building appears to have once been a hotel. On the northside of U.S. 50 is the Bainbridge Historical Center, which occupies a part of a three-story brick building.

The town hall is in a newer building. A clothing store is abandoned, but the town pantry, with a deli, offers groceries and videos rentals. A Dairy Queen is down the street.

A sign promotes the Paint Valley Jamboree featuring country music on Saturday night in Paxton Township Hall, a large two-story brick built in 1909.

We stop at Margie's Country Crafts where owner Margaret Mathews calls U.S. 50 "the biggest little highway left in America." She cites the history on its route through Bainbridge and expresses her hope that residents can become active in the preservation of the town's past.

Margie's business, which includes full floral service hasn't been opened long but her guest book already includes names of visitors from a number of states as well as Germany.

At least two annual events bring tourists to Bainbridge. The Fall Festival of Leaves, the third weekend of October, offers motorists an opportunity to view the colorful beauty of the hills of southern Ohio. Four routes - called Buckskin Hills, Red Brush, Paint Vista and Pike Lake - are recommended by festival officials, who call this part of the state "Ohio's Valley of the Kings."

Visitors can also drive through the Paint Valley hills in the spring when the dogwood trees are in bloom.

We make a note to visit Bainbridge on one of those occasions.

* * *

East of Bainbridge, corn and soybeans grow in fields with hills as backdrops. A farmer with a John Deere rig combines wheat. Old stone two-story I-frame homes that date back two centuries are off the road.

We pass Paint Valley High School - "home of the Tigers," which is in a rural area east of Bainbridge.

U.S. 50 turns to the northeast as it passes more old farm houses. One, a square two-story, its sides covered in ivy is abandoned, its past buried like those who once called it home.

The road has become more windy, the curves noted by 45 mph speed limit warnings.

* * *

U.S. 50 has become antique alley. Collectibles, gifts and antiques are available at the Old Barn Door in Bourneville, a small hamlet between Bainbridge and Chillicothe.

There are few retail outlets, but the Diary Hut promotes the "next tenderloin fry July 5."

An old, but well-maintained farmstead is at the edge of Bourneville. A cemetery, large in contrast to the size of the town, is an indication the area was once more heavily populated.

U.S. 50 continues to angle northeast toward Chillicothe, eight miles or so away. The pavement is smooth. An old double crib along side of the road is a reminder of a time when farmers pulled their wagons under roof and scooped corn to either side.

New houses along the road indicate we are approaching a city of some size. Lawns are manicured. Round bales of hay dot a field as we pass through Slate Mills, a community overlooked by Ohio map makers.

* * *

It is obvious we are about to enter Chillicothe. A huge lumber outlet is at roadside, as is a National Guard Armory. A six screen theater is open, apartment units are under construction and other businesses are nearby.

A curving hill with a 35 mph speed limit is on the approach to Chillicothe, U.S. 50 angling northeast, then southeast as it enters the city.

We note a McDonald's, a CVS Pharmacy, a Burger King, a Bob Evans and a KFC, the first of each we have seen since leaving Cincinnati. Their absences along the 90-mile route is an indication U.S. 50 has not changed much between the two cities over the decades.

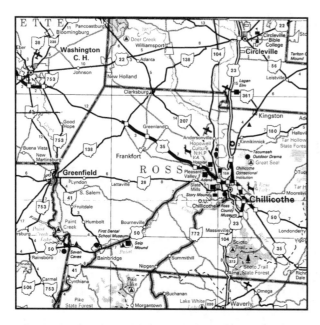

The west entrance into Chillicothe on U.S. 50 is lined with convenience stores, retail outlets, food marts, fast food restaurants, shopping centers, auto parts stores and paint shops.

U.S. 50 follows Western Avenue, then Main Street starting at the Ohio 104 intersection. A teen-age boy bounces a basketball across the road, oblivious to the cars waiting at a light. The pavement narrows to two lanes before the road passes two blocks south of the historic heart of Chillicothe.

It is obvious this is an old city, one that has taken pride in its past and cares about its present. Many residences in the older section of the city are both large and historic. So are many of the business buildings.

Chillicothe is said to be a Shawnee word for "principal town." It's a good definition for this is principal town, the largest city on U.S. 50 between Cincinnati and Parkersburg, W.Va.

It was founded August 20, 1796, by Nathaniel Massie, and Bicentennial Park is a reminder of its 200th anniversary in 1996.

It became the capital of part of the Northwest Territory in 1800 and was designated the state capital when Ohio became part of the Union in 1803. The capital remained here until 1809, when it was moved to Zanesville. Chillicothe again was the seat of state government from 1812 to 1816 when the capital was moved to Columbus where it remains.

The state's oldest newspaper, "The Chillicothe Gazette," was first published in 1802.

To enjoy downtown Chillicothe, it is recommended that visitors stroll through the area leisurely, without time limitations. There is much to observe. We chose a Sunday morning to tour the area, a time when there is little traffic. We are impressed for this is one downtown that has retained its vigor and pride, keeping its tradition and preserving its heritage.

The Old Capital District just off U.S. 50 is quiet except for some prisoners at work cleaning the area around the Law Enforcement Complex. Next to it, four columns rise at the front of the Ross County Courthouse, Neo-Classic in design and closed for business on this day of rest.

The four-story Carlisle Building is accentuated with a turret at the top. Other buildings in the area also are old, mostly two and three-story brick, all well maintained. An old hotel is now used for other purposes. The historic Majestic Theater, built in 1853 and said to be the oldest free standing theater in the U.S., is north of Second Street.

One of the city's most significant intersections is Carlisle Corner where U.S. 50 is crossed by Paint Street, separating West and East Main (which is the U.S. 50 route). To the south of Main Street on Fifth Street are the Ross County Historical Museum, circa 1838; the library, and the restored Knoles Log Home, now almost 200 years old. The Franklin House, a prairie style home dedicated to the county's women, is on South Paint Street.

There is, it seems to travelers, always something to do in Chillicothe, be it assorted festivals, musical shows, parades or fairs. Among the main events is the Feast of the Flowering Moon Festival on Memorial Day weekend.

Perhaps the best known attraction is "Tecumseh," an outdoor historical drama presented daily from early June to early September. It is a professional outdoor drama portraying the life of the Shawnee leader Tecumseh. It's a popular attraction, but perhaps a bit overstated in an effusive promotional brochure:

"Here beneath a canopy of stars, across the quiet waters and from encircling forests, a spectacle of unbelievable proportion explodes around you, as horses gallop down the hills, arrows whisper overhead in deadly flight, flintlocks bark and artillery thunders through the woodlands."

Mayor Margaret Planton acknowledges the significance of U.S. 50 to her city, its route little changed since it first linked Chillicothe to Washington and points in between. "Although not a major freeway, it is a beautiful old scenic route that connects Chillicothe with many historic attractions," she explains, adding:

"U.S. 50, one of the oldest routes into the city, is still well maintained and still important to the area's economy, history, travel and tourism. It is an integral part of our area."

Travelers planning overnight stops on U.S. 50 may want to choose Chillicothe. Motels, restaurants and shopping areas are to the north across the Scioto River on Ohio business route 23 near the Ohio 35 interchange.

U.S. 50 leaves the Old Capital District past fast food restaurants and an old business area before merging for a short distance with U.S. 34 and U.S. 23. The four-lane road through the Scioto River valley is elevated over fields of soybeans. Houses in the valley also are built on elevations to avoid high water in case of floods.

* * *

U.S. 50 again becomes a two-lane road as it resumes its route to the east beyond Chillicothe. Athens, a road sign says, is 53 miles ahead.

Farms with fine old homes line the narrow road. A square frame house from an earlier era predates the road itself. Its yard, fenced in pickets, is fronted by a "for sale" sign for anyone interested in buying a bit of history.

Nice churches rise on the horizon from time to time, beacons of hope for those within sight. Not far away is a Christmas tree farm.

We encounter the most traffic we have witnessed for miles. Ten cars, caught in a no passing zone, are behind a truck enroute toward Chillicothe. Hills lie ahead, some approaching mountain status.

* * *

The town of Londonderry extends like a shoestring along U.S. 50, its length greater than its width. Houses, fields behind them, line the road for a distance. It is soon obvious Londonderry is bigger than it first appears. An elementary school, a church, a gun and ammunition business, a market and a cemetery are along the road.

Flags fly over some homes near Londonderry, the pride of Americans in their country not limited by geography or economics.

An old two-story farmhouse is abandoned, replaced by a mobile home.

* * *

We are in entering Appalachia, an area defined by the federal government as all of West Virginia and parts of Ohio, New York, Pennsylvania, Maryland, Virginia, Kentucky, Tennessee, North Carolina, South Carolina, Georgia, Alabama and Mississippi.

Appalachia includes 29 counties in southeastern Ohio, an area different from the rest of the state in its history, geography and economy. The rugged foothills of the Appalachian Mountains may be an economically inferior area compared to the rest of the state, but its scenery is unmatched.

U.S. 50 is the economic lifeline of the area, the nearest interstate miles away. Most of the area's other narrow and winding roads remain unchanged, deterring extensive industrial development.

VINTON COUNTY

As we enter Vinton County, the scenery exemplifies the county's boasts that it offers "nature at its best."

U.S. 50 has been improved, its route changed for a short distance, but remains two lanes. Slopes of the hills are coated with green grass as we approach Ratcliffburg, a community now bypassed by U.S.50 and overlooked by map makers.

The road curves through a valley, bordered by fields in the laps of the hills. The speed limit drops to 35 mph as the route twists and turns through the Wayne National Forest that covers much of Vinton County.

Older houses dot the side of the road. A sawmill is at the foot of a hill, timber being one of the area's biggest natural resources.

* * *

The speed limit drops to 45 mph as we enter Allensville, another hill town that follows a valley. Services are underway at the Allensville Christian Church, a place of worship since 1878. A junior high school is off the road.

A sign offers "wild boar hunting" for sportsmen. A used car lot, a fixture in almost every community across the nation, is near some abandoned buildings.

A short distance away a sign - for no apparent reason - reads "Tampa, Florida, 1143 miles." It's near the Cross Creek General Store, which offers a bit of everything, except Sunday service. "Please stop again," a sign says.

On an adjoining lot, some venders are preparing for the weekly flea market, an opportunity for sellers to make extra cash and for buyers to search for collectibles as well as bargains.

Used cars and manufactured homes are for sale near a 90-degree turn on U.S. 50. A man who takes pride in his environment is picking up cans tossed carelessly to the roadside by uncaring motorists.

U.S. 50 runs through a narrow valley, the traffic protected from sharp drop offs by guard rails as it leaves Allensville.

Satellite dishes are common, giving residents the right to life, liberty and the pursuit of their favorite television shows even in areas where cable is not available.

* * *

We feel at times we are on Lonesome Road. The highway winds its way through Wayne National Forest, a scenic drive uncluttered with traffic. We can relax, slow down and enjoy the view for there are no cars behind.

The road passes what is called "Rusty Rail Ranch," a barn on one side, a house on the other.

A few cars are parked at the Lucky Star Motel as we approach McArthur. Tourists are no longer a prime source of revenue for businesses along the route now that many motorists prefer to travel on nondescript interstates.

They are the losers for this is the real America, the heartbeat of the nation.

Under construction on the south side of U.S. 50 as we near McArthur is the Vinton County High School. It will replace an old building in town that has been in use for decades. "Viking Country," reads a signs promoting the school's athletic teams.

Not far away we are welcomed to "Friendly McArthur." We will soon learn the greeting sign is truth in advertising for McArthur is a congenial place to stop.

Another sign at the Shell Convenience Store, however, may draw more attention on this day. It reads, "Happy 80th birthday Ruth Morley, You Old Fart." A few days later it will be changed to "Happy Birthday Theresa."

A cashier explains the mobile sign is a town billboard of sorts, offering a different message each day. "If someone wants to extend a greeting, we let them," she says.

We eat at the Main Street Diner, which has experienced servers, not teen-agers waiting at a fast food computer to punch in an order. "Main Street" is a morning gathering spot for town residents, a place to have coffee with both cream and conversation. A recent storm is the major topic of the day for the damage has been extensive and the inconveniences many.

The town of 1,550 residents appears lost in time, unchanged much, we suspect, since we passed through McArthur in the 1940s and 1950s. This, we hasten to add, is more of a compliment than a criticism. There are no fast food restaurants, no chain operations, no superstores that have driven mom and pop businesses from many county seat towns.

It is good to see a place that hasn't been invaded by seekers of dollars at the expense of tradition. It is a place for visitors to come to remember what small town America once was.

Instead of franchise restaurants there are places like the Main Street Diner, the Sawmill Inn, which boasts of its filet mignon, and a home-owned market. Instead of a Holiday Inn there is the McArthur Hotel.

Most buildings are brick from an earlier era, many no longer are in use. The Vinton County Courthouse, which faces U.S. 50, is fronted by a memorial to area soldiers of all wars. The jail is in an old building, not in one of the modern structures the politically correct call Law Enforcement Centers. The county library is in the downtown area as is the McArthur Village Hall.

A block off U.S. 50 are twin cinemas in an old brick building. "I Can Hardly Wait" is playing on one screen, "Dirty Works" on the other, "all seats $3."

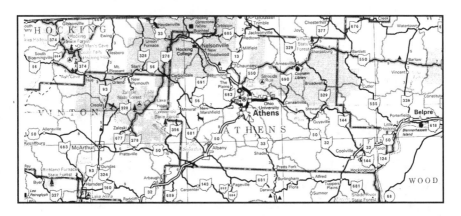

We leave McArthur, feeling better for having stopped.

* * *

East of McArthur U.S. 50 winds across a valley, then slices between hills on its way toward Prattsville. An old general store that once served the rural community is closed.

The pavement is rough as we skirt the north edge of another section of the Wayne National Forest. Poles shaped like the frames of teepees are filled with vines of string beans in a garden in a valley near a mobile home.

Prattsville is off U.S. 50, the road having been relocated to skirt the small town. The only activity is a car headed in the opposite direction.

Call U.S. 50 in this area the lonely road for there is little traffic at times. Most trucks use four-lane Ohio 32 which angles northeast on its way to join U.S. 50 up ahead.

Another general store along the road is closed, but a recycling center near the Vinton-Athens County line is in business. A pump in a field brings crude oil from deep in the earth.

ATHENS COUNTY

Just inside Athens County, U.S. 50 merges with Ohio 32, "the Appalachian Highway," en route to Albany and Athens.

"Downtown" Albany, population 800, is accessible from an exit that passes under U.S. 50 and Ohio 52. This a church town, seven are listed in the phone directory, and the parking lot of most of them are filled on a Sunday morning.

A fixture in Albany is the Albany House, a pre-Civil War home that is now a bed and breakfast with four bedrooms upstairs and what its promotional information calls a "full size indoor swimming pool."

It is said "sweethearts" from nearby Ohio University come to stay, a claim that may cause alarm for protective dads and concerns for some mothers.

Just off U.S. 50-Ohio 32, which bypasses Albany to the south, is the Country Harvest House, its only competition the Pizza Shack and a Dairy Queen, which fittingly is on Blizzard Lane.

The Harvest House proves a good choice for a late breakfast. It's a friendly place, one where the customers and servers know each other well enough to exchange pleasantries as well as barbs.

Breakfast gives way to lunch, the Sunday buffet and baked steak dinners - $5.49 each - attracting early customers as churches are dismissed.

* * *

The four-lane route toward Athens seems to have temporarily taken some of the glamour from the trip. There is little nostalgia, with little to note along the way as the road turns northeast. Athens is accessible to the east off U.S. 50, U.S. 32 ending its arc across deep southern Ohio.

* * *

Athens, population 21,265, is yesterday, today and tomorrow. It is an old town dating back to 1797. Its yesterdays date back two centuries. Its today is its role in the vitality of Athens County. Its future is the students enrolled at Ohio University.

Streets, many still paved with brick, are narrow and sometimes confusing to follow, the slow drives through the city adding to its charm. Old buildings stuck like decals on the sides of the hills make Athens seem like a city from an European setting.

Much of the charm of Athens is its scenic setting on the foothills of the Appalachian chain. Its brick streets, homes and business buildings retain the appearance of its earlier years.

Churches are old, so are most of the buildings, many occupied with businesses that cater to college students. The ancient

Houses line side of hills in city of Athens

railroad depot has been redone, a tribute to preservationists who
have kept it from falling into disrepair or erased by demolition.

It is, however, the Ohio University campus that dominates
much of the city, which also is the Athens County seat of government. Chartered by the state of Ohio in 1804, Ohio University
was the first university in the Northwest Territory.

At first glance, O.U. appears small, too small it seems for the
20,000 students on campus. But it is compact, most classroom
buildings on the 1,700-acre campus within a 10-minute stroll.
College Green, the centerpiece of the university, has brick walks
lined with trees and is on the National Register of Historic
Places. Cutler Hall, circa 1816, is a National Historic Landmark.

Like most college towns, Athens has its cluster of motels and
restaurants.

Off the U.S. 50-U.S. 33 bypass in Athens is the Dairy Barn
Cultural Arts Center, promoted as the site of international,
national and regional arts and craft events. Quilt National, a
quilt show, attracts entries from around the world.

* * *

Ohio 32 ends at Athens, but U.S. 50 again turns east as a four-lane road for a short distance, then narrows to two lanes. The road at this point is being widened to a four-lane divided highway and construction is under way, limiting access to the houses off the extended right-of-way. The route again angles to the southeast as we enter another section of the Wayne National Forest.

A silo stands forlorn, any trace of a house or barn gone with past. Slabs of concrete have been uprooted, heaped in unsightly piles, making way for new pavement.

Construction ends and we again are on a two-lane winding section of U.S. 50. "Rough road," a sign says, as if motorists need to be reminded.

We are in a somewhat desolate area, one that could be in Indiana, Kentucky or Tennessee, for most states east of the Mississippi have common characteristics. Cattle graze on the grassy hills, the meadows lush from recent rains.

* * *

Canaanville, a small town in the valley, is almost inaccessible because of the road construction, the giant concrete barricades now hiding the houses beyond. The town, however, is a reminder of the earlier years in Appalachia.

Consider this from an Athens County book by Elizabeth Grover Beatty and Marjorie S. Stone:

"As mines opened in southeast Ohio, numerous company towns - some small, some with hundreds of houses for miners - strung out along creek beds and ridges. The houses were usually all alike, either a four-room cottage or shotgun style - three rooms in a row, front to back.

"Many different ethnic groups arrived as the mines expanded, making the area's population more diverse than surrounding agricultural communities. Some company towns would consist of one nationality, but others were a combination of native born Swedish, Finnish, German, Italian, Hungarian, Slavic, Welsh and English."

The coal industry was often controlled by outside interests, which reinvested little of the profits for improvement of the area. Coal was a major industry, but one that fluctuated wildly with booms and busts. When oil took away much of the need for coal, some of the coal companies abandoned the communities they had created, leaving workers without jobs. In a 30-year period from 1940 to 1978, an estimated three million people left the Appalachian region.

* * *

We are in the Hocking River valley as we near the community of Guysville. It is a town that appears to be a ghost of its past, unlike a picture we have seen on the Internet.

That scene on a Thanksgiving postcard showed Guysville of 1908, a year when the Chapman Brothers' Store was open, a time when farmers brought live chickens to town in coops to be traded for staples. A grain mill was in town then, allowing farmers to swap wheat for flour.

Not much remains in Guysville. It now is a hamlet of homes off U.S. 50, its past exceeding its present. We find the name of a Guysville restaurant, tastily named the Sweet Lix, but a telephone operator says the number no longer is in service.

Despite the lack of businesses, a number of homes remain in the little town where Ohio 329 joins U.S. 50.

* * *

South of Guysville we enter another area where the road is being widened to four lanes. The route improves in a short distance and cars pick up speed. But traffic soon slows, then stops behind a long line of cars and pickups.

A mudslide - following heavy rains - has closed the road here in the Hocking River Valley. Up ahead the muck is being scooped aside by earthmovers.

We are in no rush, but most motorists are, this being the era of impatience. They fume, stew, then turn and head back toward Athens. A few take off to the north over rural roads only those who know them would dare take. Others hike back and forth on the pavement, unhappy that Mother Nature has delayed their trips.

A fire truck arrives to hose off the highway. After 35 minutes we resume our travel, more aware of the irritability of Americans in the late 1990s.

* * *

Old feed mill in town of Coolville

Near the town of Coolville U.S. 50 merges with Ohio 7 and becomes a four-lane road.

It is soon obvious Coolville is an old town. It has a library, a grocery, a school (Troy Township), a few other businesses and a barbershop that looks like a picture from out of the past. It also - on this day - has water, lots and lots of water. And it has a compassionate citizenry.

The Hocking River is out of its banks and lowlands are flooded. Residents of a nursing home in nearby Arcadia have been evacuated and are being temporarily housed in a Coolville Church. Volunteers are helping care for the evacuees, giving their time and energy to those in distress. In small towns, one person's woe is another person's concern.

Much of the town is out to offer help. A town fire truck is standing by as are some rescue units in case more evacuations are needed.

Near the evacuation area is an ancient two-story brick, its windows boarded. A white-on-blue sign on an ancient brick structure reads: "Coolville - Building Community - One Block at a Time." The healing of a disaster is today's building block for the community.

Over a hill, is an old mill, part of Coolville's heritage. The book, "Getting to Know Athens County," reveals Simeon and Herman Cooley, pioneers in the milling industry, built a dam across the Hocking River in 1815 to power a flour mill, grist and sawmill.

That original mill was replaced in 1882, then destroyed by fire in 1922. Its replacement, still at river's edge, appears to out of business although a Purina Chow sign remains.

A distillery near the mill allowed farmers, who chose, to sell their grain for conversion into spirits. On this date, however, the spirit is in the compassionate hearts of the people of Coolville.

Ohio 144, which follows the Hocking River, is under water.

* * *

The divided four-lane U.S. 50 and its Ohio 7 companion turn east at Coolville as it passes through scrub timber into the community of Torch. An antique store is closed, an old roadside motel out of business. Torch is only a wide spot on the road en route toward the Ohio River.

WASHINGTON COUNTY

U.S. 50 runs near the Ohio as it skirts the river town of Little Hocking, population 600.

Except for a couple of stores and a Napoli's Pizza outlet, which allows its customers to order via the Internet, there doesn't appear to be much activity in Little Hocking.

The section of U.S. 50 northeast from Little Hocking continues to follow the Ohio River as it twists its way toward Belpre and Parkersburg, W.Va.

A road now marked Ohio 618, which appears to have once been U.S. 50, leads into Belpre, the new U.S. 50 now taking a path to the north as it skirts the city.

* * *

The name Belpre is a contraction of "Belle Prairie," a French word for "beautiful meadow." It may have appeared to be that - a beautiful meadow - two centuries ago when it was created as the second oldest settlement in the Northwest Territory.

Town historians say Belpre was settled in 1789 by about 40 associates of the New England Ohio Company, who built a fort called "Farmers Castle" for protection against the Indians.

The city of 6,800 residents is high above the Ohio River, some of its streets flooded, nevertheless, on this day after heavy rains to the north. A tractor is pulling a fire truck, stalled in high water, toward its station.

The view of the valley below is still spectacular from a vantage point at the Belpre Lions Club building. A township office is nearby as is an old brick house overlooking the bluff on the Ohio side of the river.

The area is on the Belpre Historical Tour, one that passes the site of the first Universalist Society of Belpre, founded in the 1820s as the first congregation of the Universalist Church of Ohio.

Belpre also is the site of Lee Middleton Original Dolls, a factory listed among "Time Magazine's" great America roadside attractions. Lee Middleton is deceased, but production of her dolls continues, the factory still a tourist designation for toy collectors.

* * *

Back on the highway, Ohio 7 continues to follow the river toward Marietta. We continue on U.S. 50 which crosses a north-south bridge over the Ohio River before turning back east as it enters West Virginia. The 175-mile journey across southern Ohio is complete, but we will return in a few days to retrace our route.

CHAPTER 3
WEST VIRGINIA

Had there been no Civil War, there may have been no West Virginia. Residents, loyal to the United States, chose to form the new state and join the Union on June 20, 1863, rather than remain a part of Virginia and the Confederacy.

West Virginia was a poorer, but freer society, the terrain more rugged. What farms that existed were small in contrast to the plantations of the Virginia from which it separated.

The heart of the Appalachians are in West Virginia, making it the Mountain State, its people sometime known as Mountaineers.

U.S. 50 across the state had its origin in 1827 when the Northwestern Turnpike became more than a dream. The road, planners said, would connect Winchester (Va.) to Parkersburg, create competition with the National Road (later known as U.S. 40) and provide a shorter route to the west.

The route became known as U.S. 50 after the federal government adopted a uniform numbering system in 1925. East-west roads would have even numbers, north-south routes odd numbers.

WOOD COUNTY

Parkersburg, population, 33,00, is a river city, a place where the Little Kanawha joins the Ohio. Established in 1811, it was chartered in 1820, a hub of commerce 305 miles west of Washington, 145 miles southwest of Pittsburgh and 192 miles east of Cincinnati.

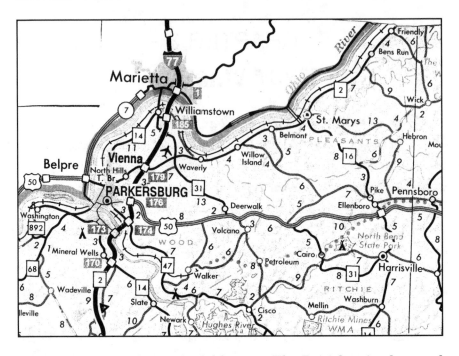

The area is rich in colorful history. The British gained control of the region in 1763 after the French and Indian War. In 1770 a party directed by George Washington journeyed down the Ohio to survey the region, where development began in the 1780s.

An economic boom came with the drilling of West Virginia's first oil wells in 1860. The region continued to develop as an industrial center in the late 1880s when the gas fields to the east were tapped and industrial plants began using natural gas instead of coal as fuel.

U.S. 50 meanders through the old sections of Parkersburg over narrow streets, many of the stoplights old and sometimes difficult to see in bright sunlight. A trip through town takes some time, U.S. 50 being a mix of four lanes, three lanes (one lane for left turns) and narrow two lanes. Most of the route is lined with businesses, fast food outlets, restaurants and car sales lots.

A fixture on the route is Colombo's Restaurant, a Parkersburg dining attraction since 1954. It proves a wise choice for dinner, the pasta dishes unequaled, the service good, the servers congenial and the atmosphere agreeable.

Owner Jimmy Colombo, we learn, also is Parkersburg's mayor, so we choose to let him tell us later about his home town. He answers the phone himself at the mayor's office, his unrehearsed comments about U.S. 50 and Parkersburg as precise as if written by a public relations adviser.

"For us," he says, "U.S. 50 is a major highway, an important route that traverses our area of the state. Economically, much of what we have today is because U.S. 50 has created a lot of opportunities for the city."

We mention the narrow route U.S. 50 takes through sections of Parkersburg. He agrees, but adds: "Funds, fortunately, are now available (late 1998) to allow us to widen the road to four lanes through the city."

Like us, Mayor Colombo enjoys traveling Route 50. "I've traveled U.S. 50 many times and found it fun to drive. It provides a great view of nature as it runs through the hills of West Virginia. People who do a lot of traveling seem to be leaving the interstates to return to routes like U.S. 50. We've noticed at the restaurant that more people are taking the road as they cross this area of the country."

The Chamber of Commerce couldn't promote Parkersburg any better than Colombo. Listen to him: "This is a very pleasant community, its greatest asset its people. They are friendly . . . always ready to help one another. It is a wonderful place to live and raise a family because of a low crime rate, a good educational system and stable and growing employment opportunities."

So, tell us mayor, what should visitors be certain to see when in Parkersburg:

"First of all," he says, "Blennerhassett Island." The Blennerhassett Island Museum is at the site of a historic mansion with extensive gardens. It is said to have been there that Aaron Burr plotted with owner Harman Blennerhassett, a wealthy Irish immigrant, to establish an empire south of the Ohio River. Their arrests ended the scheme.

"And Fenton Glass, which is at Williamsburg (about six miles from downtown Parkersburg) is another place that should be seen," Mayor Colombo adds. It's a family-owned business, one whose art glass is known throughout the nation. Fenton Glass items are often seen on TV shopping channels. And its operation in Williamsburg is an attraction for many bus tours that travel through the area.

Other glass making businesses, we will learn, are ahead at places like Ellenboro and Pennsboro.

* * *

U.S. 50 crosses under I-77 at the edge of Parkersburg and heads east, the road a newer four-lane section. The terrain is rugged, the traffic light. We see no towns, no houses, for some miles.

Four lanes of divided highway will continue toward Clarksburg, 77 miles to the east. We pass through the community of Dallison. Only a building that appears to once have been a general store is in sight.

The road, its access limited, slices through the Appalachians in this area of West Virginia. Building sites are few and homes are fewer. This is a road to enjoy the beauty of the terrain. It is a drive free - at least for now - of tailgating semis on hurried trips to distant destinations.

RITCHIE COUNTY

We enter Ritchie County, rich in history as are most West Virginia areas.

North Bend State Park, named for the horseshoe curve in the Hughes River, is off U.S. 50 to the south, a place to fish in streams, swim or picnic. The park is on the North Rail Trail which extends 72 scenic miles. Its 12 tunnels and 32 bridges make it an enticement for hikers, bikers and equestrian riders.

Ritchie County, formed in 1843, was named for Thomas Ritchie, a Virginia journalist. Jessie and Elias Hughes along with Col. William Lowther explored this region to the Ohio River in 1772 and Hughes River was named for them.

For motorists on U.S. 50 there are vistas to the south, east and north. At times, hills soar over the road; at other times the road runs along ridges equal to the mountain tops on the horizon ahead. No houses are visible and billboards are conspicuous by their absence. It is a welcome sight, this view unobstructed by man-made advertisements.

Steam rises as if sent through chimneys from the depths of ravines deep in the woods, but the air is clear and pollution is miles behind or beyond.

Roads off U.S. 50 have names like Bear Run, Bonds Creek and Way Station and motorists can only guess at what lead to their designations by the pioneers who settled in the area.

We have not seen a service station, a restaurant or a single roadside stop for miles. That changes when a school, modern and neat, appears on a hill not far from the Ellenboro exit.

* * *

We enter Ellenboro over what was once U.S. 50. A motel no longer is busy, the road having bypassed it to the south.

A sign proclaims we are in Ellenboro, "The Town of Glass. Established 1803." Eighteen businesses are listed on the "Welcome" board.

Ellenboro's Town Hall is in a small one-story building. The Fire Department promotes bingo each Thursday starting at 7 p.m. It's a way to raise money without raising taxes. A manufactured homes operation is in town as is a hand blown crystal glass factory.

Near a recently-flooded creek, a woman sweeps water from her produce/retail business. She isn't complaining. "A lot of other businesses were damaged worse than me," she notes, well aware of the hardships of her neighbors. As a new merchant she is trying to make enough sales to get a retail beer license, which are based on the amount of grocery sales. Beer, she adds, can add to her customer base, attracting those who might not otherwise stop.

Like all towns, Ellenboro has seen change. "There isn't as much work in the glass plants as there once was," she explains. "One glass plant, plus one that is a lot smaller are all that are left."

The annual Ellenboro Glass Festival is the second weekend in July, "a family event honoring the local handmade glass industry." Its agenda includes horseshoe pitching, arm wrestling, tugs of war, fiddle contests and carnival rides.

Motorists, who once passed through Ellenboro, now speed by on relocated U.S. 50. Much of the tourism trade is gone and the glass work has declined, but the town remains, the residents - on the surface - content in their isolation.

* * *

We are in the valley of the boros. Up ahead on the old section of U.S. 50 is the town of Pennsboro, population, 1,280. "Welcome to Pennsboro," greets a message from the churches of the area.

Part of the Pennsboro Speedway, a small dirt track, is under water, the storm oblivious to a sign that reads: "We are Pennsboro Proud." Clean up work is under way from the flooding at the Dollar Store and the IGA.

The Jones Feed Store - "groceries and hardware" an unusual combination - is a reminder of the general stores of mid-century that dispensed a variety of merchandise. A John Deere and New Holland dealership is an indication that there are sizable farms in the area. A battery shop, U-Haul Rental, an auto parts store and a cabinet company are in town.

A marker informs visitors about the Webster House, circa 1800, now known as Stone House, which was built shortly after 1800. The walls of the house, two feet thick, are flag stones of various shapes and sizes held together by cement and mortar. It was for years a stage coach inn, the only house between Clarksburg and Parkersburg. It also was the site of Ritchie County's first post office, which opened in 1820 when James Martin became the postmaster.

* * *

We soon notice that West Virginia counties, where employment opportunities are few, are eager to attract new industry. Two industrial parks are within a few miles of each other.

Many of the towns are clustered in narrow valleys, the hills above leaving businesses little room for parking space.

* * *

The town of Toll Gate, also on the old section of U.S. 50, is a short distance east of Pennsboro. Residents are working in groups to clean homes after the North Fork River rampaged through the hamlet. It is obvious that sections of the road have been under water.

A small sign notes "Toll Gate 53," a reminder of a time when travelers paid a fee to travel along the route.

A few homes have gardens on small plots on land between the creek and the hills.

DODDRIDGE COUNTY

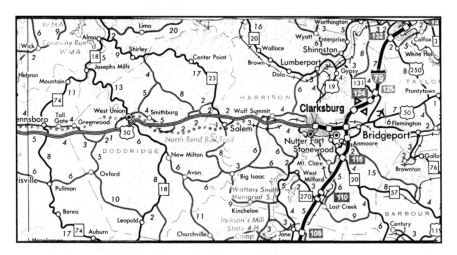

The old route returns to the relocated four-lane U.S. 50 at the community of Greenwood, another hamlet where homes are scattered along a creek. An old motel in the small town looks now to be divided into apartments. A deer processing station seems to be the only business, except for the Out Post which offers, a sign says, "Weekend Entertainment."

* * *

A few farm houses are off the road. An Exxon Station is open for motorists. But that changes quickly when we again enter an expanse without either homes or farms. The new route has isolated the little towns that once dotted U.S. 50.

We notice a few oil storage tanks, indicating some wells are in the area.

* * *

West Union, at first glance, looks like a town anchored in time. It has changed little over the years, its appearance a reminder of how the area looked on a trip almost 60 years ago.

U.S. 50 bypassed the town in the 1940s and was relocated again when the four-lane route to the south was finished in the 1970s.

This is an old town, its charm based in its history and its reflection one of a past that no longer exists in many areas of the country. West Union remains unchanged, still much like it was when motorists traveled through the town on what was once U.S. 50. The streets are narrow, barely wide enough for two vehicles to pass. Drivers who want to reach the courthouse must negotiate hills to reach it.

In population, West Union is one of the smallest county seats in America, the last census counting 830 residents. The head count for all of Doddridge County is just 7,000, maybe a few more if it has gained in population in the 1990s.

The three-story Victorian Romanesque Courthouse, which opened in 1903, looks from a distance like a castle on a hill. A limestone base is topped with red brick. Two conical towers accentuate the front.

Both the business area and the Courthouse are high on a hill, overlooking the creek and the valley below. The streets are not only narrow but short, their terminuses determined by the hills and valleys. Old buildings, indications that West Union was once a busier place, are three-story bricks. Most of the first floors are occupied with businesses for this still is a trading center, there being no cities of size between Parkersburg and Clarksburg. A senior citizens center and the Doodridge County Fitness Center also are in the heart of the town.

It is soon obvious this is an interesting - and friendly - town. One where no visitor is long a stranger. We learn this when we walk into the Doddridge County Museum across the street from the Courthouse.

Six or eight volunteers are at work, turning what was the county's 60-year-old jail into a historical center whose dedication is just two weeks away. The jail became available for the museum when a new regional incarceration center opened.

"You folks want to look around the museum?" we are asked. "We have a lot of interesting things to see," one of the volunteers insists.

We hesitate, but it's difficult to turn down an invitation from those who take pride in the history of the places where they live.

"It (the tour) won't take too long," jokes Bill Calhoun, "unless I lock you in a jail cell upstairs and lose the key." Calhoun is a walking encyclopedia, already familiar with almost every item, which isn't surprising when he mentions he is an antique buyer and seller.

Most items, some as old as the county, have been donated. A religious room has ancient pulpits from both Methodist and Baptist churches. "You can tell which is which. The Baptists had a little jug setting next to pulpit," Calhoun joshes, letting us guess what the jugs supposedly contained.

On display are old farm tools, dating back decades. So is a slip, a big scoop with wide handles steered by man and pulled by horses to move dirt, the kind we recall being used to rebuild U.S. 50 back in Indiana six decades ago.

A military room is crowded with war memorabilia, dating back before the Civil War, the conflict which led West Virginia to leave Virginia and become a separate state in 1863.

Other item have come from doctors' offices, barber shops and an old bowling alley that once was in town. On display elsewhere are pictures of all West Union and Doddridge County high school graduates dating back to 1932. The tour continues, room by room, each filled with history of a county's role in the creation of a nation.

Calhoun shows us a copy of an original map of the Northwestern Turnpike, the route reaching across West Virginia to the Ohio River before West Virginia was a state.

"A lot of U.S. 50 just followed that trail," Calhoun says as his hand sweeps across the route of the turnpike. It is obvious he is sentimental to the road and doesn't like attempts to continue to remove it from small towns.

"I'd like to shoot the people who are changing U.S. 50. I love to drive the road. Whenever I go to Washington (D.C.), I drive U.S. 50."

Thanks to Calhoun, the hour has been well spent. "We can stay here all night if you can spare the time," another volunteer adds, meaningfully.

Mansion type home across from West Union Courthouse

Calhoun gives us his business card, saying, "Stop and see us if you are out this way again." He can count on it.

* * *

We stop on the street near the museum to admire an old home that appears to have once been a mansion. A passerby notices our curiosity and volunteers:

"It was called Stuart Mansion, the home of C. J. Stuart, owner of one of the original banks in the county, one that went under during the depression. It stood vacant for most of my childhood until someone bought it about 15 years ago."

It now is in need of repair, much of the luster gone from its days as the mansion on the hill.

* * *

We wind our way down into the valley, cross a bridge over a creek (called Piggin Run on our map) onto a section of old U.S. 50 and take a long look up the hill toward the Courthouse and business area. It is a town that has reached the 21st Century without the invasion of giant discount stores, fast food restaurants and chain outlets.

Like the museum, it is a town that has preserved its heritage. We drive out of history into the present.

* * *

Old U.S. 50 to the east follows Rock Run Creek toward Smithburg, another small town whose residents are working together to clean up after the flood.

First named Smithton for its first postmaster, Francis Marion Smith, the town became Smithburg in 1924. Not much remains except the old depot, now owned by the Doddridge County Historical Society, a church or two, the hint of an old general store and a few houses that sit on a hill above the creek.

HARRISON COUNTY

We return to four-lane U.S. 50 and continue east before taking an old section of the road past a National Guard Armory and soccer fields into the town of Salem. Tourist cabins that once housed travelers are at the west edge of town, reminders of earlier trips on the highway.

Salem, it appears, is strung out along on the side of a hill following the old road as it snakes its way toward the business district.

The food is home cooked and good, the oatmeal not microwaved, at Moore's Restaurant in the heart of Salem's business district. Business is good, although the tourist traffic has been gone since U.S. 50 bypassed the town of 2,050 back around 1970.

Unlike other towns, parking meters are still in place and overtime violators are fined. This is a town that can use any extra cash it an get. The lead story on this date in the "Clarksburg Exponent" details Salem's need for cash to repair streets damaged by a contractor who installed sewer lines.

Any financial woes, however, will be forgotten for a few days the first weekend in October when Salem observes its annual "Apple Butter Festival." A brochure promises: "Something for everyone. Old fashioned apple butter making. Spicy apple butter slowly simmered over an open fire. Canned right on the spot. Take home a kettle full of memories."

Salem is the site of Fort New Salem, an assortment of log structures that represent frontier settlements. A number of annual events are held at the fort to give visitors a glimpse of what pioneer life was like in the Mountain State.

Old U.S. 50 eases northeast out of Salem past a Methodist Church built on the bank of the hill and separated from the road with iron railing.

"Thanks for visiting Salem," a sign says. The pleasure is that of those who have stopped.

* * *

Back on four-lane U.S. 50, a row of houses, off to the north, appear to be planted on the sides of a hill over a valley. A section of the old, narrow and winding road leads to Wolf Summit, another town that stretches out along a creek.

An Oddfellows Hall in good shape, unlike many IOOF Lodges, whose members no longer are active. An old store that once catered to U.S. 50 traffic is out of business. A post office remains.

* * *

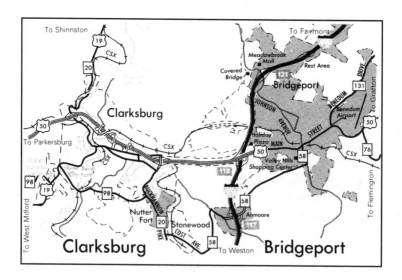

Clarksburg is the first city of size we have seen since Parkersburg, 77 miles to the west.

U.S. 50 enters Clarksburg from the west and it is soon obvious it is a city bigger than its 18,100 population.

It is the home of the expansive United Hospital Center staffed by ninety physicians and 600 nurses. The Johnson Veterans Administration Medical Center provides care for veterans from twenty-six counties.

Its diversified industries are an attraction for workers from both the city and surrounding areas. It, too, is the business center of an eight-county north central West Virginia area of 220,000 residents.

From a distance, much of the city appears to sit in a saucer ringed by wooded hills, the elevations beyond creating a post card setting.

It is an old town, one older than the nation itself, its history rooted deep in America's past. George Rogers Clark and John Simpson are said to have camped here in 1764 before heading west. The first settlement followed in about 1785 and the names of the first settlers are still noted on a city marker.

To observe Clarksburg's history and note its significance as an economic center, it is best to drive a short distance south of U.S. 50, find a parking spot and walk down Main Street. There is much to see, a lot of history to absorb on the sidewalks along narrow streets fronted by historic, and well preserved, buildings.

The sidewalks are crowded at noon on a fall day as many of the 7,000 downtown workers relax on lunch breaks from jobs at the Harrison County Courthouse, federal offices, a publishing company, banks and other businesses.

At the Courthouse, opened in 1932, markers note the site of Randolph Academy, 1850-1885, and a supply depot of the Union Army, 1861-1865. It was here Gen. George McClellan had his headquarters until the battle of Bull Run. Also noted is the fact that Clarksburg was the birthplace of Gen. Stonewall (Thomas J.) Jackson, who earned his nickname at the Battle of Bull Run.

A visitor soon learns that preservation of history is a Clarksburg industry, its portentous buildings bookmarks on the faces of time.

Among the impressive edifices is the Courthouse itself, art deco in design, its buff limestone and steel frame on a granite base stretching nine stories high. Unlike courthouses, it is not on a square and appears more like an office building than a seat of county government.

A block away is the Empire Bank, whose charter is the city's oldest. Its first floor portal is accentuated with Corinthian columns, its top level embellished with bracketed cornice, which architects say gives it a Renaissance Revival theme.

Impressive, too, is the 1853 Christ Episcopal Church, Tudor Gothic in design, the words, "The Lord in His Holy Temple," noting its role in the spiritual values of the city.

Most of the downtown buildings reflect a time when workmanship exceeded the build-it-quick, open-it-fast construction techniques of the late 1900s.

Oak Hall, for example, has a facade with 18 arched windows, each third window having brick pilasters. The Goff Building actually is a twin structure rising from one base, its Renaissance Revival architecture covered with brick made in Clarksburg. The 10-story Union National Bank towers over the business district.

Clarksburg's future may be as significant as its past. The new FBI Criminal Justice and Information Services center will eventually employ 3,500 workers. An 800-acre industrial park is attracting new industry and shopping centers are continuing to grow.

This area of West Virginia seems alive and well.

U.S. 50 passes new developments as it continues east past the Interstate 79 intersection, one whose quadrants are sites for chain motels, restaurants and convenience stops. One of only four interstates in West Virginia, Interstate 79 slices to the northeast from the southwest.

* * *

Bridgeport, population 6,800, is close enough to be a twin city to Clarksburg. It's a suburb to the east, the division line between the two neighbors roughly I-79.

Bridgeport, a trading post since 1764, is still a commercial center, the site of a huge shopping center near the intersection of I-79 and U.S. 50. It is at this point that U.S. 50 again becomes a two-way road, exceptions being a third lane for passing on its route through Bridgeport.

In some sections of Bridgeport, U.S. 50 is barely wide enough for two cars to pass between those parked at both curbs. The road passes an old walk-up Dairy Queen and the Bendum Civic Museum as it continues east into a less populous area of the state.

* * *

Beyond Bridgeport, U.S. 50 turns northeast through mostly undeveloped hilly terrain, then passes through a community called Maple Valley. The road is narrow and winding, appearing to be unchanged, except for some occasional repavement, since it was built decades ago

TAYLOR COUNTY

There are no houses visible from the road as U.S. 50 passes through a valley. Traffic is light, which is good for the pavement is narrow and there is little room for driver error. The isolation changes. Houses are built on the sides of the hills, blanketed in dark green grass. A nice farm is ahead, its house and outbuildings on a knoll offering a good view of the valley below.

The scenic view back to the west offers an excellent postscript to where we have been.

We enter the hamlet of Belgium, which isn't on our map, a tiny spot at road's edge with a creek that runs through it. Belgium is a satellite dish or two, a few houses, a sweeping curve and a tavern.

U.S. 50 drops down into Pruntytown, which is big enough to be on the map, but too small for census takers to list its population.

Pruntytown has a few houses, a Baptist Church, a BP Convenience Store and a restaurant called the Stagecoach, and an auto dealership. It also has a night spot, one that seeks exotic dancers via a sign that reads "Now Hireing." We hope spelling is not a qualification for the positions. A motel no longer is a motel, its one-time westbound customers now opting for rooms ahead at the Clarksburg-Bridgeport interchange.

* * *

We are in Civil War country, a fitting place for a burial site for men and women who died in that war and others that were to follow. We enter the West Virginia National Cemetery, located between Pruntytown and Grafton. There is no indication a funeral is in progress. We are at the peak of the graveyard on the narrow road before we see services for a veteran are being conducted at the chapel.

There is no place to turn back. We turn off the car engine and watch the services, embarrassed for having interrupted the solemn and dignified occasion. A member of the firing squad accepts our apology and graciously explains our intrusion went unnoticed.

The view from atop the cemetery offers the panoramic splendor to the north, east and south. The grounds are well maintained, a fitting and deserving resting place for veterans who fought for causes in which they believed.

The West Virginia National Cemetery, one of 115 located in 39 different states, is not the only one in the area. The Grafton National Cemetery, which dates back to 1865, reached its capacity in 1961, leaving burials to be conducted at the newer one west of Grafton.

The National Cemetery Administration, which oversees the cemeteries, is charged with providing dignified burials and lasting memorials in the cemeteries that are maintained as national shrines.

It is fitting that Memorial Day is a major observance in Grafton. It is then that thousands of Taylor County children, each dressed in white and clutching a floral bouquet and a small American flag, march through the Grafton business district to the National Cemetery. At the cemetery, each child, learning lessons in patriotism and remembrance, gently places the flowers and the flag on a grave.

The parade has been conducted since 1869 when Maj. William Ballon asked that citizens set aside the day to join the Civil War veterans in the observance of "Flower Strewing Day." Grafton later became known as "Memorial City," a title it has earned and is entitled to keep.

* * *

Two West Virginia recreation areas are near U.S. 50. Tygart Lake State Park is to the south, Valley Falls State Park to the north.

* * *

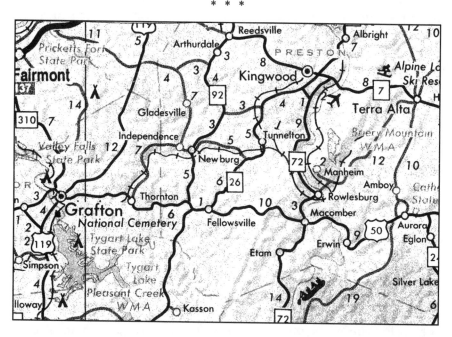

En route into Grafton from the west, U.S. 50 makes a horseshoe bend, bringing signs that limit speeds to a 25 mph maximum. A section of the road has been redone to reduce the sharpness of one of the turns. The road then runs straight for a distance before narrowing as it rings the side of a hill.

At the edge of Grafton a welcome sign notes the city of 5,500 is the home of the International Mothers of Day Shrine.

Grafton, county seat of Taylor County, has a hospital and an assortment of businesses, most of which are independent operations, the area's population not large enough to attract a super-store such as a Wal-Mart or Kmart.

The Dairy Queen is a reminder of the past, serving customers from a walk-up window. Other food franchise are McDonald's and KFC, but most restaurants have names such as Hometown, Biggie's and Four Corners.

A marker on the north side of U.S. 50 notes an early Grafton cemetery: "About 500 graves of early Grafton settlers dated 1857-1917 are in an old cemetery on land given by Sara Fetterman to the St. Augustine Catholic Church. Headstones include names of Irish and German immigrants. Buried here is Thomas McGraw, B&O Railroad construction supervisor and local merchant and father of John T. McGraw, lawyer, banker, politician and coal and lumber developer."

Grafton obviously is a town that remembers its dead.

* * *

East of Grafton, U.S. 50 remains two lanes and narrow as it descends a mountain, guard rails protecting eastbound motorists from the bluffs below.

In the community of Thornton, a convenience store provides a place to buy snacks, gasoline, beer, wine and lottery tickets, gambling having become a major revenue source for state governments. West Virginia is a participant in Power Ball, a form of gambling that brings commonality to the states in which the lottery can be played.

* * *

[It was somewhere in this area that the author's dad decided to stop for the night on a drive east back in 1940. A man of the Great Depression who knew the value of money, he was attracted by a "Cabins - $3.95 and up" sign. He may have overlooked the "and up" part.

["This should be a good place to stop," he surmised. Minutes later, he returned to the car, stomping mad, mincing words. "Damned sign is a lie," he stormed, his Buick throwing gravel as he sped back onto U.S. 50 and headed for cheaper accommodations, explaining:

["I'm not spendin' $5.45 to rent a cabin for the night when the confounded sign says it is $3.95."]

Further east we pass a drive-in theater, one of a few that remain open, most having disappeared with the coming of VCRs and home movies. The road, it seems, continues time after time to drop down one incline to rise onto another. Satellite dishes are common, the area too remote, too thinly populated, to make cable financially feasible.

A section of the road has been repaved as it drops down and passes Maple Run Community Church, the name apparently taken from the creek to the rear.

The road, wider in some areas, zigs and zags as it cuts through the rugged terrain and winds its way up hills, down hills and through valleys. To the south, a foot log leads over a creek to a house on the opposite side.

PRESTON COUNTY

The road has not been repaved as it has been back to the west. It is well to observe the 25 mph speed limits warnings, the 90-degree turns allowing little margin for speed. There are few semis and no tailgating, leaving us to enjoy a drive others might detest.

At Evansville, an unincorporated village, an insurance office no longer is open. An abandoned house is in sharp contrast to nice homes along the south side of the highway.

East of Evansville we note the first cattle we have seen in miles. The grass is plush, the grazing area ample.

"Your highway taxes at work," a sign notes at a road improvement project.

Evansville, a crossroads community, has a restaurant, a gasoline station, a salvage yard and a church. The road continues to wind as it leaves Evansville, passing homes that are separated from the road by a creek.

Again the speed limit drops as we enter the hamlet of Fellowsville, which has a church, a few houses, a restaurant, a volunteer fire department and a school in the valley. A park is a short distance from the town.

* * *

We enter a wooded area, the branches of trees on each side of the road reaching out to meet, forming a tunnel of sorts for the cars to pass through. Guard rails protect motorists from deep drop offs.

The second semi we have seen in miles is headed in the opposite direction as we ascend Laurel Mountain, its elevation high enough to pop our ears.

Suddenly we are at the top, the trees end, a farm appears and a vista opens across the woodlands below. It is an unexpected change, but it does not last. What goes up goes down and Laurel Mountain begins to drop as it passes a Christian Church. Hairpin turns limit speeds to 15 mph where waterfalls cascade down the mountainside after a rainstorm.

A store from out of the past is anchored on the eastern down slope. It is Cool Springs Park, a fixture at the location since 1929. "Souvenirs of all states," a sign boasts. It's a restaurant and dairy bar with unlimited "want-it-find-it" merchandise: Candy, hunting and fishing licenses, Indian moccasins, hardware, sweat shirts, flags, hats, maple syrup, molasses, jewelry, sorghum, honey, apple butter, groceries, stove pipes, sport goods, camping supplies.

Cool Springs is a Wal-Mart without the name. The "park" in its name come from the setting where old farm tractors, rakes, plows, steam engines and hay loaders are on display.

* * *

At McComber, we leave U.S. 50 and drive a short distance north where a sign greets visitors: "Welcome to Historic Rowlesburg, Established 1858."

An official West Virginia travel guide recommends a stop at the Curiosity Shoppe in Rowlesburg, but this venture we are on is an odyssey, not a shopping trip.

Rowlesburg is a mountain town of 650 residents that extends for a distance on the slopes of the turbulent Cheat River. The Cheat is flooded, the water almost as dark as chocolate, looking thick enough to slice if not for the swift current.

There will be no raft rides on the Cheat on this date, but that will change as soon as the water recedes. The free flowing river is one of the most popular streams for rafting in the eastern United States and Rowlesburg is the site of the Cheat River Outdoor Center.

For non-rafters, the area is a good place to bike, hike, hunt, fish or climb.

* * *

Back at McComber, U.S. 50 follows the Cheat Valley where a garden remains high enough above the river to avoid the flood.

The road turns south where it crosses the Cheat, then follows the side of a mountain along a southeast twist, the traffic protected from the flooded river by guard rails.

At river's edge is Erwin, an unincorporated community at the side of a mountain with a few houses. In a garden, string beans look healthy as they vine their way up teepees formed by four poles.

The road turns back to the east as U.S. 50 leaves the river's side, the pavement still hugging the mountain side as it ascends Cheat Mountain.

At the top of the 2,746-foot elevation, cattle are socializing instead of grazing, the grass lush enough to have sated their appetites. Farms with nice houses, barns, silos and corn fields are unexpected sites along the plateau.

Higher mountains are off in the distance to the north. The top of Cheat does not peak, it flattens out for miles, offering great views - and surprises - on it lofty perch.

One surprise is a town, "Welcome to Aurora, founded 1787," a sign greets us. It is a community of nice homes, a park and a few retail outlets as it extends along the highway.

A historical marker reveals that Aurora was established as Mt. Carmel by the Rev. John Stough, who operated the first grist mill. The first church, Salem Evangelical Lutheran Church, was organized in the 1790s.

At the Fairlea Motel and Restaurant, two customers treat us as friends, talk about the weather, their jobs, tell us the motel no longer expects tourists, having rented rooms to permanent residents.

One of the men suggests we take a side trip to the south over Stemple Ridge Road, which angles off U.S. 50 from the motel. "You won't be disappointed," he promises.

He is right. The views across the farms and mountains are spectacular as the rural road winds southwest. The elevation soars above that at Aurora. There is no traffic, just peaceful vistas that open before us, a view few strangers to the area ever see, one sure to offer a brilliant picture of fall beauty when the leaves turn. It's a five mile trip into the unexpected.

When we return, the man who has told us about the trip is back at his home on Stemple Ridge. We thank him for the travel tip.

* * *

A view from road of Old Stone Tavern

Cathedral State Park, a nature area with woodland walking trails, is on U.S. 50 where the road starts its decline from the elevation.

Another surprise awaits us on the downside of the mountain. "Old Stone Tavern," reads a sign to the north. The tavern, built by Henry Grimes around 1825, is barely visible in its location below the road.

We find a place to park off the road, then descend the steps to what once was a tavern - and an inn - on the Northwestern Turnpike. A watering trough out front is hollowed in a log from a huge tree. It is the kind that horses could drink from at the end of a day's travel.

The doors are ajar and we walk in. Wood is burning in the fireplace and the fixtures look as if they might date back to 1825.

We are appreciating the atmosphere when Melanie Myers enters from another room. She does not mind our intrusion for we have not realized the museum also is home to her and her husband, Paul.

Pioneer Henry Grimes, it seems, recognized early that money could be made from travelers along the Northwestern Turnpike that later would become U.S. 50. He turned his former kitchen into a tavern, the first in the area.

The bar was in a room with a bed where guests could sleep, the cost of lodging dependent on how many people shared it for the night. A trap door, allowed the barkeeper to escape to another area of the house after locking up the liquor, lest guests awaken with a thirst for more drink.

Virginia's legislature (this being a part of Virginia at the time) set maximum fees that could be charged by an "ordinary," which is what a tavern was then called. Operators had to provide bedding, a meal of soup or stew and a place for animals to be kept overnight.

Prices at one time, Mrs. Myers tell us, were five pence if no more than four men shared a bed. If more than four people used the bed, the price was four pence.

It was the custom, she adds, for any late arrival to awaken the sleeping guests and introduce himself.

"Sheets were to be changed every six months, whether they needed to be or not," she says, a smile crossing her face.

A tavern owner could make extra money by renting a pipe, the smoking kind. Clay pipes, in fashion at the time, were fragile and often broke during travel.

The inn, known at times as the "Red Horse," at other times as the "Old Stone Tavern," remained an inn for decades before it was bought by an Amish farmers, who lived behind it.

It now is a weekend retreat for the Myers, who bought the property in 1987 and have sought to retain the ambiance of the late 18th Century, Mrs. Myers explains.

"Before we erected the museum sign, a lot of people thought it was a restaurant, a tavern or a bed and breakfast. That brought all kinds of experiences, not all of which were positive," she adds, as she leads us on a tour.

The floor of the "central room" is still covered with 18th Century linoleum and about 90 percent of the wood remains from the original construction.

Some modern conveniences - range, indoor plumbing, microwave, indoor plumbing, dishwasher - are disguised with wood that looks original. "I wanted some conveniences . . . I like to cook on the hearth but not after a day of hard work," Mrs. Myers admits.

The house, she adds, was vacant from 1940 to 1960, when Lewis Stemple bought it and began restoration. It was placed on the National Register of Historic Places in 1973.

The restoration is not complete. "We hope to continue with the work and to eventually operate the place as a small living history farm," she explains.

She is as unhurried as we are. An hour has passed quickly. "Any charge?" we ask.

"No," she said, then adds, "we do accept contributions to keep the place accessible to visitors." It's a modest cost for a lesson in history.

"If you get back this way, stop in again," she says as we begin the walk back to the highway. She can depend on that.

CHAPTER 4

MARYLAND

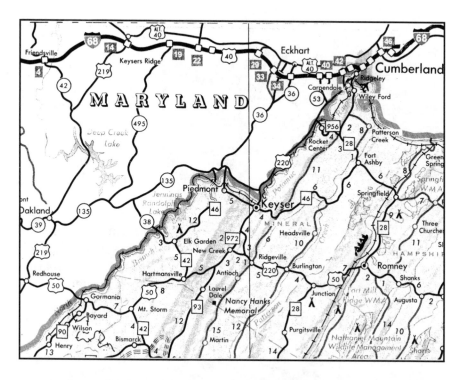

A short distance east of the Old Stone Tavern a section of West Virginia's rugged border is divided by a gap that is filled in by a triangular wedge of Maryland. The border of Maryland, the seventh of the original thirteen states, are marked by a north-south boundary line on the west and the North Branch of the Potomac River on the east.

As we have noted at other hill country farms, houses sometimes are on one side of the road, barns on the other. The U.S. 50 pavement is rough as it passes this sometimes forgotten section of Maryland, the state's political clout far away in Annapolis. Suddenly the terrain flattens and farm country reappears as we arrive at Redhouse, an intersection of U.S. 50 and Maryland 219.

U.S. 50 is called the George Washington Highway in Maryland, it's route across the state's triangle just 12 miles long. The southern tip is seven miles to the south of Redhouse, which is a service station and a house or two.

Steve Knett's store in Redhouse, Maryland

Steve Knett owns the only business in Redhouse, the gas station and grocery with a variety of merchandise. He greets us warmly, there being no customers.

"Things are going well. Staying pretty busy," he says cheerfully, upbeat after 13 years as Redhouse's only full-time entrepreneur. If he feels isolated from the rest of Maryland he does not complain.

"Oakland, a bigger Maryland town, is nine miles north, so we're not really alone down here at the point. It's true," he says, "we are in the middle of nowhere, but I'm a Marylander and happy to be one.

"A lot of people coming out of D.C. think they are lost when they learn they're in Maryland. They don't realize it dips to the south at this point where it is crossed by U.S. 50."

He isn't certain how the crossroads community got its name. "I've been told there once was a house on the opposite corner that served Civil War soldiers who referred to it as the red house."

The soldiers are long gone and the area is now occupied by farmers, coal miners and timber cutters.

Redhouse looks to have once been a busier place. Across the street is what was the Chimney Corner Dining Room, "choice steaks and fried chicken." Nearby is Grandma's Attic, "something for everyone," but it closed on this day.

* * *

East of Redhouse, still another barn is painted with a "Chew Mail Pouch Tobacco sign." Amish quilts are for sale not far away.

U.S. 50 scales Backbone Mountain, its 3,360-foot elevation making it the highest point on the Maryland state road system. The mountain offers a splendid view back to the west, a panorama of the mountains opens to the south. Both scenes are pictures to preserve in the memory of the mind to be viewed again at a later time.

The Backbone Mountain Restaurant at the side of the road is in ruins, destroyed by fire.

Surprisingly, fire hydrants appear along the road in this area that is far from any sizable towns. Chickens peck for food morsels on the pavement for there is not enough traffic for them to learn roads do not make safe dining tables.

CHAPTER 5

WEST VIRGINIA - AGAIN

MINERAL COUNTY

U.S. 50 crosses the North Branch of the Potomac River and again enters West Virginia. The old, old town of Gormania is near the river. The Gormania Trading Post, in a three-story building at roadside, looks like it might once have been a roadside hotel. A convenience store is open as is a garage.

Union High School is to the east, a restaurant beyond. Truck traffic is heavier as the road passes through farm land.

We have noticed there are no welcome station, no stopping spots with restrooms on U.S. 50. Its users are forgotten travelers.

* * *

Mount Storm is another unincorporated neighborhood that accompanies the road for a distance. At the Mountaineer Motel visitors are advised: "Last chance, lowest rates. Single person $24."

The Mount Storm post office is at the top of the mountain. An antique shop is open, so is Getz's Market. A sign indicates the community has an active Lions Club.

We are en route down the mountain, aware of a nine percent slope when we stop at Getz's Restaurant on the north side of U.S. 50.

A friendly waitress learns we are tourists and explains we may not be allowed to continue our descent. "Police," she says, "have blocked the road in what is called a crisis situation in which a gunman is being sought."

A regular customer, listening in, jokes, "What'd he do? Hold up a tree?"

"Maybe someone has gone wild," says another, seemingly unconcerned, then adds, "Ain't nothin' down there, anyhow, 'cept two or three houses."

It is a big topic of conversations. "A hostage situation," one surmises. Another man says he heard it was a shooting, then explains the detour options if we are stopped.

This is a fun restaurant, the conversation is easy at mid-afternoon, a place for the locals to relax. A man walks in and says he has been splitting wood, "Oak, locust, maple."

He quickly changes the subject when he spots a waitress. "What did you do? Take another vacation," he jests, then adds, "I haven't seen you for a week."

She brings our order of apple dumplings with ice cream, $1.50 per serving. "Excellent," we tell the waitress as we pay the bill.

"The cook made them," she says giving credit where due.

[A few days later en route back to the west, we again stop at Getz's restaurant. We order pancakes this time and get three as large as the plate, 12 inches in diameter.

[A supervisor for a telephone cable that stretches across the mountain has stopped for coffee. He talks about his job, the snakes - copperheads and rattlers - he has seen in the forests that cover the hills and hollows. The chances of getting poison ivy, he says, are greater, though, than being snake bit.

["You have a good trip," he says as we leave, another positive mark on the hospitality of this rural area.]

* * *

[Our memory unwinds to 1941. We are on a family trip to Washington and have stopped for gasoline somewhere in the area where we are now.

[My nephew enters the store section of the station and invests a nickel in a slot machine. He wins an amount, now forgotten, but not more than $2. It is a big sum in that year for a boy of eight and he is too pleased not to share his good news.

[It is a mistake. Dad, who knows the value of money and a one-armed bandit's odds, gives him a $3 verbal lesson. The nephew keeps the money. It is years before he again wagers on a game of chance.]

* * *

The road continues its decline down the mountain into Hartmansville, another town anchored to the highway. It has a Methodist Church, an abandoned store building, one of the first outdoor basketball goals we have seen in miles, a few homes and lots of mountain scenery.

A mile away we meet the roadblock the folks back at the restaurant told us to expect. A volunteer firemen explains the detour we need to take, then volunteers what he has heard. A jealous lover has slain his girl friend for dating another man.

He does not know the full story, we will learn later.

The drama of the real story is reported in newspapers the next day: "A Keyser man was taken into custody following a manhunt that ended when a police sharpshooter disabled the suspect's weapon with a clean shot from 100 yards."

The excellent aim of West Virginians has been known for decades. But a shot that can disable another gun from 300 feet exceeds the legend.

The suspect, sought after a gun battle at a motor home, had hidden out in the rugged, wooded terrain. State police said the dispute was "domestic in nature."

* * *

We return later to Hartmansville and resume our journey east.

A scenic overlook off Saddle Mountain offers an awesome view from a turn in the road, mountain tops visible in the distance. The pavement is good, but the road is winding, its curves to be taken at no more than 25 mph.

A settlement in the valley below gives no indication of its name, if it has one.

The Clayville United Methodist Church is in an old building, a modern edifice not a requirement for a religious community. A few cars are at a motel, which appears to be a mom and pop operation that has withstood the competition of nationally-promoted overnight lodging.

Homes are perched on side of hills with satellite dishes. A Union service station is abandoned as is another station not too far away. An old covered bridge crosses a creek, a road passing through to a house beyond.

"Timberlake Estates - prime building sites," an ambitious developer advertises.

Ridgeville is small, a wide spot in the road, but a country club appears almost in the middle of nowhere. An old native stone inn is for sale, its days of glory gone with the traffic.

* * *

It is the surprises, the unexpected, the non-promoted places that make traveling interesting. One of those sites is in the town of Burlington.

Service station museum in Burlington

It is the service station museum at the south edge of U.S. 50, a picture from out of the past. It is a station with a roof that extends over the gas pumps out front.

The museum is closed, but its old tin signs are reminders of an earlier time. A sign notes, "This is not a going business." No matter! It stirs memories of the 1940s when such stations were common, when full service meant an attendant would pump the gas, clean the windshield and check the oil.

Two gravity flow pumps, the kind on which a handle pumped gasoline into a glass cylinder from which it flowed into tanks of cars and trucks.

Signs for different makes of gasoline - Texaco, Fire Chief, Amoco, Gulf, American - are tacked onto the museum's front.

Another sign notes: "Authorized Service - Whippet and Willy's-Knight genuine parts."

A Coca Cola box remains out front from an era when soft drinks were cooled in water, the moisture flipped off and the lid jerked off at the opener on the side.

Ed Weaver's 1923 TT Model truck with a wooden cab, the crank in place, is parked in the bay that extends out to the gas pumps. The spokes of the wheels are painted red. A sign asks visitors not to touch the vehicle for it is a man's prized possession.

An old tire is near the truck, flowers growing in it. A church pew out front is a reminder when men gathered at such stations to wile away the hours and enjoy a double dip cone of Genteria, "the ice cream of all ice creams, excellent for health."

Posted on a window is a December 6, 1933, front page from the "Baltimore Sun," the main headline noting the end of prohibition.

The museum we learn later is on the National Register of Historic Sites. It also has been cited by the West Virginia preservation office in recognition of significant contribution to the preservation of the Burlington Historical District. The citation is merited for this is a reflection of an earlier time when travel was slower and businesses were independent, not incorporated.

Out front at a house near the museum is a separator, the kind with a handle that turned to create a centrifugal force which divided cream from whole milk. It adds another glimpse of nostalgia to the scene.

* * *

Patterson Creek flows behind the station, making Burlington typical of West Virginia towns that grew up along streams. Some boys, maybe 10 or 11, are building a dam in the stream, probably to catch minnow, fish or frogs, boys being boys wherever they may live.

A sign promotes an ice cream social, one of the old-time social events that still exists in small communities. Another annual event is the old-fashioned Apple Harvest Festival the first weekend in October.

A gift shop, pizza place, several other businesses and the volunteer fire department are along the road.

HAMPSHIRE COUNTY

A two-story log house is along the road as are scattered farms
as we approach the community of Junction, which isn't much
more than an intersection of U.S. 50 and West Virginia 288.

Some farm fields are in the laps of the valley, hills beyond
forming the backdrop. Another barn is painted "Chew Mail
Pouch - Treat Yourself to The Best." Mail Pouch signs of our yesterdays are the television commercials of our todays.

Farms are larger as the valley widens on the approach to
Romney. One is designated a National Bicentennial Farm, its origin dating back prior to 1776.

* * *

Hampshire House Country Inn in Romney

Overnight accommodations await us in Romney at the
Hampshire House Country Inn, which a promotional brochure
boasts will offer "the luxury of the 1800s, the comforts of today."

It is truth in advertising. Owners and innkeepers Jane and Scott Simmons see to that. We choose the Hampshire House's Whitacre Room, named after a former owner of the home that dates back to 1884. The furnishings are even older. An attached bath and an alcohol burning fireplace are added attractions.

A full country breakfast in the dining room is the choice of each individual guest, and made to order by Mrs. Simmons and served on this date by the Simmons' 10-year-old grandson, Michael. Michael, up from his home at Wilmington, N.C., to spend a couple of weeks, is enjoying life on the family farm when not serving diners.

* * *

Romney is near the South Branch of the Potomac river and is called West Virginia's oldest town. It is one that is storied in history and folklore. It also is county seat of Hampshire County.

And it was the center of a continuous struggle between the north and the south in the Civil War. An historical marker elaborates:

"Setting astride the natural invasion route from the Shenandoah Valley to the Potomac and B&O Railroad, Romney was sought by both armies. No great battles were fought here but during the war the town changed hands 56 times."

Romney was incorporated in 1762 and later platted as a town by Lord Fairfax, a vast landowner

Literary Hall on U.S. 50 in Romney

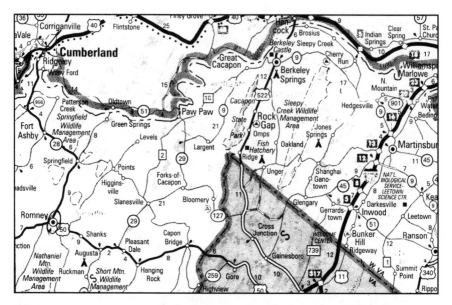

whose property extended over much of the area. Not far away was Fort Pearsall, built in 1756 as a defense against Indians.

There is more to Romney than war. This is the site of Old Literary Hall, the original home of the Literary Society of Romney, formed in 1819.

Despite a population of just 2,000, Romney is the business, government and shopping center for Hampshire County. It is quiet, though, the carillon at a church adding to the serenity, making the town a more peaceful place than it was from 1861 to 1865 when two armies made it a battleground.

On an opposite corner from the Hampshire County Courthouse is an old three-story building with a triangular front, the kind entered through a door at its corner. An old inn with a balcony over its porch remains. Not far away on U.S. 50, which passes the courthouse on its way through town, is a two-story original log cabin.

The West Virginia School for the Deaf, established in 1870, is on U.S. 50 at the east edge of town.

* * *

Those interested in more history may want to observe the Fort Mill Ridge Trenches, called the best preserved Civil War trenches that still remain. Another Romney landmark is the

Hopewell Indian burial mound (500-1000 A.D.), the largest east of the Ohio River.

Visitors to the area from May through October may want to drive a mile north of Romney on West Virginia 28 to board the Potomac Eagle, a three-hour railroad excursion through some of the state's most scenic areas.

* * *

A small shopping center, a fast food restaurant and Hampshire High school are at the east edge of town.

U.S. 50 curves around the side of South Branch Mountain, hugging its rock face. A church is at the top of the mountain, the elevation 1,462 feet.

In the community of Shanks, old gas pumps remain at what once was a general store. An old house is lined with flower pots, pride in one's property not dependent on wealth.

Traffic slows to 40 mph as U.S. 50, with no berms on either side, winds into a valley. Houses are scattered along the lowland. Another abandoned store and gas station is across the road from one that remains open.

Not far away is another "Mail Pouch Tobacco" sign, but this one is different. It's on the side of an abandoned house, not on a barn.

East of Shanks, U.S. 50 is three lane, one for passing, as the road heads up another incline.

* * *

Atop Short Mountain is the town of Augusta, site of the Hampshire County Fair. It appears to be a small business center with churches, service stations, a branch bank, a restaurant, a funeral home in what looks like a plantation style home, a few stores, a used car lot and an antique outlet in a farm barn covered with signs.

Play houses are offered for sale by a woodworking entrepreneur.

* * *

Two miles east is Pleasant Dale. A video store, a hair salon and a few houses are along the mile-and-half between its town identification signs.

A sign on the highway reads simply: "Bible - Basic Instructions Before Leaving Earth."

* * *

We stop on the down slope of the mountain east of Pleasant Dale at Haines Market, a roadside stand offering "fresh fruit in season."

It is more, however, than a fruit stand. Its merchandise ranges from country hams to antique fruit jars with a zillion other items in between.

We are greeted by a nudge from a black and white Collie and a "mornin'" from a shopper who is leaving with fresh peaches.

The operator identifies himself as "Haines," using his last name as an identifier as do most men his age. "Stanley," he answers when asked his first name.

Haines is a man weathered by age and the hardships of his generation, his face as creased with gullies as the hills of his native West Virginia.

He agrees he has a wide assortment of items. "A bit of everything," including he admits, "a lot of junk." Name it and he has it - shovels, tires, auto parts, plumbing, old magazines, license plates from years past.

"Been here about 10 years. When I first started I just sold fruit. My boy owns most of the other stuff," he explains, adding: "He had a shop in Pennsylvania. When he moved to Arizona to be with his children, I got his junk. I sell a right smart of it."

Haines, "born and raised back over in the hills," spent 35 years elsewhere, before coming home to the places he knows best.

If interstates have taken vehicles off U.S. 50, Haines hasn't noticed. He says, over the sounds of a lumbering semi, "I think traffic through here, including them big old trucks, is heavier than it was before interstates opened."

We leave Stanley Haines to serve his next customer. His "junk" may be another man's treasure.

* * *

U.S. 50 again enters an area where it snakes between a stream on one side, a mountain bluff on the other. Guard rails become a driver's security blanket. The road ascends another mountain.

We stop at another reminder of the past, a one-time oasis of sorts for motorists with overheated cars. A marker tells the story:

"In 1938 the West Virginia Road Commission contracted the W. W. Keister family of Romney to build this fountain to provide water for tourists and their overheated autos. In 1952, the spring was declared unsafe to drink and the fountain was abandoned in 1992."

The Hampshire County Historical Society began restoration, but the work has not been completed. A historical society's work, it seems, is never done.

* * *

U.S. 50 drops sharply down from the peak of Cooper Mountain, elevation, 1,607feet, as it dips toward Lost North River, which it crosses at the village of Hanging Rock.

As we approach Hanging Rock we pass another barn painted in "Mail Pouch." Big tobacco may be faulted for the addiction of users, but its advertisements have preserved some barns that might have faded into oblivion if left unpainted.

Flags fly at modest homes, patriotism not exclusive only to the rich. Satellites are common in this cableless area that is fertile territory for PrimeStar and other systems bringing additional channels to television viewers.

* * *

We remain in a historically significant section of U.S. 50 as we reach the Cacapon River.

A marker notes that in 1784 George Washington proposed the Northwestern Turnpike as an all-Virginia route to the Ohio River. Authorized in 1827 and started in 1831 it remains a monument to the skills of its engineers.

* * *

The highway crosses the bridge over the Cacapon and enters the town of Capon (pronounced Kay'pun) Bridge, not far from the Virginia Border.

Capon Bridge is the only sizable town in the area, certainly the only one with a McDonald's Restaurant. It also has a Romney Bank branch, a huge fire station and rescue unit, an American Legion post, two service stations, a drug store, car dealership, car wash and pizza outlet. Except for employment opportunities, it is a self-sufficient community.

An employee at McDonald's refuses to guess how many residents call Capon Bridge. "I just know it's a lot bigger than Highview, the town of 30 people where I live. In Highview you can stand at one town limit sign and see the other."

We mention that it's unusual to see a McDonald's in such a small town. The employee agrees, then adds, "But it is nice to have something here. We serve a big area plus a lot of people stop here as they pass through on their way to work at jobs in Winchester (Va.).

"Days like this are kind of slow, but it picks up in the evenings when there are baseball games and other events."

Across the way is a house, maybe 72-80 feet long, two-story, eight windows across the front on each level. It appears to have been an inn dating back to the time of the Northwestern Turnpike. It's not more than 40 feet from the center of U.S. 50. Wood is stacked to the side ready to be burned in two fireplaces.

A tired motorist can only imagine the pleasure of listening to the rain on the tin roof after a long day on the road.

"It's huge, big enough for a bar and a dining area with a dance floor," another McDonald's worker explains, then adds, "When I was younger it was a restaurant and an inn, but that was before it became just a residence. It has a lot of room for just two people (the current residents)."

Down the street, a funeral is underway at the mortuary, some of the mourners arriving by cars, others on foot from nearby homes. The size of the crowd indicates the town has lost a respected resident.

* * *

Capon Bridge's town limits have been expanded along U.S. 50 up part of Baer Garden Mountain, elevation 1,101 feet. It is the last in the Allegheny Chain.

More and more trucks are on U.S. 50, this being an area where timber is a major economic resource.

We have reached Virginia, the border, fashioned when West Virginia opted to leave it back in 1863, extending jaggedly north to northeast.

CHAPTER 6
VIRGINIA

Aristocracy is alive and well and living in harmony with Middle America in Virginia, a land of plantation mansions and modest homes.

This is a state of fox hunts, horse shows, apple blossoms, unexcelled scenery, the glory of the Shenandoah Valley, the majesty of the Blue Ridge Mountains, and a bulk of American history.

Two-lane eastbound U.S. 50 enters the state sparsely traveled at the down slope of the Allegheny Mountains. It leaves the state traffic-laden through Arlington, looping around Arlington National Cemetery en route through the nation's capital on its way to Maryland.

In between is a cross section of the nation, the powerful and the powerless, the wealthy and the not-so rich, the pretentious and the common folk.

* * *

Chances are the name Claudius Crozet means little, if anything, to travelers on U.S. 50. But it was Crozet who would have a lasting impact on the roads of Virginia.

Crozet, a French artillery officer under Napoleon Bonaparte, later taught at West Point, and became in 1823 Virginia's principal road engineer. One of his major accomplishments was the Northwestern Turnpike.

The idea for the road emerged in 1827 when the state sought a profitable trade route toward the states beyond the Ohio. Progress was slow, mainly because its supporters preferred a circuitous route through the most populated towns.

It wasn't until 1831 that the Virginia legislature voted to borrow money and build the turnpike with a minimum 12-foot

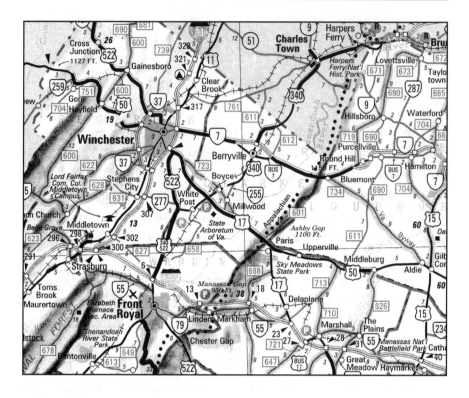

width. It was to extend from Winchester to a point on the Ohio River, the location to be determined by Crozet.

Crozet created one of the major roads of its day, one that stretched across what was to become West Virginia (then a part of the state of Virginia) to the Ohio River. The course he designed is followed basically by the U.S. 50 of today, still considered to be one of the most - if not the most - important non-interstate road in the United States.

* * *

In Virginia, U.S. 50 is a four-lane route from near Gore through Winchester to the town of Paris. It narrows to two lanes through the hills and past plantations to Fairfax, then widens to four and later six lanes as it enters the continuous suburbs of Fairfax County and becomes Arlington Boulevard.

FREDERICK COUNTY

We cross the border from West Virginia. The view from the elevation is a scene to remember. The air is clean, the skies clear, the horizon ahead seemingly endless.

"Welcome to Virginia," a sign reads, a warning added: "Buckled seat belts is the law."

The Skyline Tavern is near the state line, a last chance or a first chance for a drink, depending on the direction a motorist is headed. A motorist in a hurry becomes our tailgate, being more accustomed to the twists and turns on the down slope than we.

We approached the town of Gore, which, as far as we know, has no relationship to Vice President Al Gore. It is here that U.S. 50 again becomes a four-lane divided highway on its southeasterly route.

* * *

Gore is another hamlet bypassed by U.S. 50. Its older section is off relocated U.S. 50 to the south. A convenience store is there, so is an ever present beauty salon, but there is little else in the way of business. An old motel now appears to be used for more permanent housing.

Near Back Creek, which runs through Gore, two Winchester and Western Railroad locomotives are rusting on a section of track.

Gore, though, is like a lot of other towns, additional proof that business and government go where the traffic is. The Gore Post Office and a branch bank are out on relocated U.S. 50.

Off the north lanes a short distance from Gore is a marker in remembrance of one the area's more noted natives:

"This house, built in 1858, was the childhood home of novelist Willa Cather from 1874 to 1883 when she moved to Nebraska with her family. The house was the setting of the final chapters of her novel, 'Sapphira and the Slave Girl.' She was born near the community of Gore, then known as Back Creek Valley."

* * *

Traffic becomes heavier as we near Winchester. A motel attempts to lure motorists before they arrive in Winchester and its clusters of hostelries. This one is independent. "American Owned and Operated, Rooms $19.50 Up," a sign read.

The highway in this area is well maintained. A few cafes and restaurants along the route indicate we are nearing a heavier populated region.

In the tiny hamlet of Hayfield an old house has been abandoned and there is little activity.

Billboards clutter the road sides on the approach to Winchester. Small businesses, used car lots, auto repair shops, service stations and small motels are along the route.

* * *

Winchester will prove to be another city that appears larger than its 22,200 population.

The Winchester Medical Center, a huge facility for a town this size, is at the west entrance. The divided highway, tree lined and well maintained, offers an impressive introduction to Winchester as it passes a spacious middle school.

The road, sometimes hard to follow because of turns, narrows to three lane, one for left turns, as it enters the heart of town. Old houses, some mansion-like, all well-maintained, front on the road.

A historical marker notes the city was first called Frederick Town. Another notes the second Battle of Winchester during the Civil War.

Back to the west, the hills loom in the distance, a reminder of the mountains we have left behind.

The road becomes two lane near the business district and passes an old railroad depot, restored as the home of the Winchester Little Theater. A Farmers Market is open not far away.

We park, this being an area too steeped in history for a stop-and-go. A longer and closer look is required. Winchester, we soon decide, is yesterday and today looking forward to tomorrow.

It's called "the crossroads of the Civil War," but Winchester's history began decades earlier. Much earlier. The Old Town Development Board boasts of its "250 years of history and architecture."

The city was settled in 1731 and officially founded in 1744 by Colonel James Woods, making it the first British town west of the Blue Ridge Mountains. Four public lots were conveyed to the town by Woods from land he bought from Thomas Lord Fairfax. Fairfax could spare the land, being that he owned 5,282,000 acres that stretched from the Rappahannock and Potomac Rivers to Chesapeake Bay.

[Fairfax, sixth Baron Fairfax of Cameron, was a Scottish peer born in Kent, England, in 1693. He inherited from his mother, the daughter of Baron Thomas Colepepper, governor of Virginia, one-fourth of the entire colony of Virginia. He built a home in the Shenandoah Valley and despite his wealth and his land he remained a loyalist during the War for Independence.]

It was here, under the direction of Fairfax, that George Washington began his surveying career. It was in this area that Washington directed the building of Fort Loudoun and had his headquarters as commander on the Virginia frontier. And it was from here Washington was elected to the Virginia House of Burgesses in 1758.

It is here in the old section of Winchester that Lord Fairfax, called the "proprietor of the Northern Neck of Virginia," has his tomb on the grounds of Christ Church Cathedral.

And it was Winchester that was taken and retaken 72 times - 13 times in one day - as the Union and the Confederacy fought, again and again, to control the strategic location.

The county's original log courthouse, 40 feet square, was finished in 1761. It was far different structure than the spacious Greek Revival Courthouse that now sits on the same site, the government and the population having greatly exceeded the original needs. Like the Courthouse, the Frederick and Winchester Judicial Center is in an imposing building.

In the heart of Winchester is the Old Town Welcome Center, which is a good place to learn about the city and to begin a walking tour.

Not far away is a monument to Confederate soldier from Winchester and Frederick County "who faithfully served the south."

George Washington's Office Museum is a reminder of where the first president worked while directing construction of Fort Loudoun, an outpost on what was then the Western frontier of the English colonies. Another museum, Confederate Gen. Stonewall Jackson's headquarters, is in the small home where he lived while stationed in the area. Across Piccadilly Street, is the headquarters of Union Gen. Philip Sheridan.

Downtown Winchester is a busy place on this day. The sidewalks are crowded and office workers are being served at noon by ice cream and hot dog vendors in the open Old Town Mall.

It is apples, not ice cream or hot dogs, that add to Winchester's heritage. The city is home to the Shenandoah Apple Blossom Festival and Apple Blossom Mall is near the interchange of I-81 and U.S. 50. The festival is another event that stems from George Washington's days in the area. It was Washington, who as a landlord, required each of his tenants to plant four acres of apples.

Extensive orchards still surround Winchester, creating a vista of beauty when the blossoms appear in May. The Winchester Rotary Apple Harvest Arts and Crafts Festival is in September when the apples ripen.

It is soon obvious that Winchester is a big little city, one whose past is written in the 250 years it has been the focal point of Virginia's northwestern triangle.

* * *

We leave Winchester heading southeast on U.S. 50. The view is good, the Shenandoah River is ahead, the Shenandoah Valley beyond, the Blue Ridge Mountains their backdrop to the south.

It is a nice scenic drive. We are just 60 miles away from the congestion and political intrigue in Washington, but the peaceful setting makes the distance seem a weekend away. Conversation lulls for these are miles to appreciate in silence, scenes to store in the mind like snapshots in an album.

On U.S. 340, a mile or so north of U.S. 50 (which also is marked U.S. 17 in this area) is the State Arboretum of Virginia. At least 850 varieties of trees, plants and flowers are on the 170-acre grounds. It is worth a side trip for such opportunities to observe nature are rare.

CLARKE COUNTY

We are entering horse country as we drop down into the Shenandoah Valley. The Shenandoah River is peaceful, calm and clear, far different than the dark, brown turbulent uncontrolled water of the mountain rivers and streams to the west.

The U.S. 50 bridge is wide and smooth, a far better crossing than the makeshift ferries that preceded highway construction.

A sign notes - as if motorists need to be told - that the Shenandoah is a scenic river. "Scenic" seems an understatement for a river of song and story, romance and war.

Beyond the river, U.S. 50 rises toward the Blue Ridge Mountains. It is an area without the visual pollution of giant billboards that often detract from the view elsewhere.

We remain in an area once owned by Lord Fairfax and visited often by George Washington. It was here that families, later granted land, came bringing slaves, establishing plantations and fostering their love of fox hunts.

Despite the ravages of the Civil War, some old plantation homes remain. Much of the land is now covered with apple and peach orchards that replaced the wheat fields of the Civil War era.

* * *

A marker along U.S. notes the significance Ashby Gap played in the Civil War. An important signal station just to the south was an important signal station, used at times by both armies from 1861-1865.

Ashby Gap, elevation 1,000 feet, was named for John Ashby, an early settler who is said to be the first person to haul a hogshead (a volume that could have ranged from 62 to 140 gallons) of tobacco through the gap.

Ashby's Tavern, a circa 1740 house, was once a stopping place for pioneer travelers headed west through the gap, which still offers a panoramic sweep across rolling hills and farms below.

It is in this area that hikers on the Appalachian Trail cross U.S. 50 as they head north or south.

* * *

We turn off the road to the north and drive past a horse farm into Millwood, a small town. The Burwell-Morgan grist mill, built in 1782-85 and continuing to grind grain until the mid-1900s, is now owned by the Clarke County Historical Association. It is a treasure worth preserving.

The Burwell in the name is Nathaniel, a wealthy earlier settler of the area not far from the Shenandoah. The Morgan is Gen. Daniel Morgan, a Revolutionary War leader who is said to have supervised construction and directed operations of the mill in its first years of operation.

Another reminder of the past is a hardware store that appears unchanged despite the Lowe's and Furrows elsewhere.

Not far away a roadside motel has surrendered to the Ramadas, Holiday Inns and elegant bed and breakfasts. It has become a row of apartments.

* * *

U.S. 17 leaves U.S. 50 at Paris, another old town, its main street called Federal. Republican is another street, but we do not find a Democrat street if there is one.

A landmark in Paris is the 1819 Ashby Inn, conveniently located for those who golf, hike, ride, collect antiques, enjoy horse shows and desire a respite from a more hectic life. It is a noted get-away destination, especially from the pressure of government jobs in Washington, a quick trip from the nation's capital.

A sign near the inn reads, "Speak to the cow, as if she were a lady." We have yet to grasp its meaning.

A farm is for sale at the edge of Paris. Not far away an old two-story Federalist style home appears to comfortable in its peaceful surroundings.

* * *

[Memo to historical groups who post markers for travelers. Too many are placed at the side of narrow roads, leaving no room for motorists to pull off and read them.]

FAUQUIER COUNTY

Stone fence lines U.S. 50 in Virginia

"Preserving agriculture," says a sign introducing Fauquier County. It is a county that also is preserving a more urbane way off life.

This is horse country, one where fox hunting is still a sport. U.S. 50, now two lane, is lined with old houses, huge, well-maintained.

Rock fences from plantation days line the road. East of Paris, a stone fence stretches continuously for 2.5 miles, a half dozen or more estates, beyond.

The properties have names. Along the way we will note Lazy Acres, Hawthorne, Stoneleigh, Brook Hill and Stonebridge. Some are named after people, some for places, some for things. Among such titles, plain old "Goose Creek" seems as if it needs a more elegant name to equal its surroundings.

Goose Creek and its four-arched Stone Bridge, now bypassed by U.S. 50, was an important site in the Civil War. It was at the bridge that J.E.B. Stuart's Confederate forces held off Union soldiers in fighting that was a prelude to the Gettysburg Campaign.

* * *

It is well that U.S. 50 is two-lane through the area. It has helped preserve a quality of life, keeping the area from being overrun by rampant development and the increased traffic that would follow.

And U.S. 50, free of billboards, fits the terrain and its surrounding. Construction of a wider road would leave scars on the environment that would never disappear.

* * *

Upperville is a mixture of elegance and simplicity. Many of its homes and businesses are old, the buildings made of native stone dating back almost two centuries. Many extend out almost to the berms of U.S. 50, which is so narrow on some blocks that parked delivery trucks limit traffic to one lane.

Two churches stand out. Trinity Episcopal Church, which faces the road, was designed by architect H. Page Cross and built in 1955. Most of the stone and wood was shaped by men from the area who designed and forged their cutting tools. The pulpit, pews

Entrance to Upperville United Methodist Church

and other furnishings have sculptured ornamentations, showing the care given by parishioners turned craftsmen.

The church has been host to its Annual Hunt Country Stable tour for 40 years, the proceeds used for its outreach programs. The self-driven tour permits participants to see farms and stables and, a promotion brochure promises: "Views of undulating hills with stone walls, board fencing, grazing horses and cattle, early Federal style farm houses, colonial roads sunken with over 250 years of use, woodlands and pasture where one can glimpse clusters of historical buildings."

It is a May event that attracts visitors from Washington, 45 minutes away.

Just south of U.S. 50 is the much older United Methodist Church, the tombstones in its adjoining cemetery dating back to the first decade of the 1800s.

An old type service station is at roadside it Upperville. It is another of the kind at which travelers along this route stopped when the automobile was new and cross country travelers were few. A roof extends out from the brick building to cover one bay and the pumps. The pumps are modern, having replaced the kind with glass cylinders at the top which allowed gravity to carry fuel through hoses to vehicles.

A bell signals our entrance through the door into the station, which could be a setting for a Norman Rockwell picture. The inside is little different than the stations of mid-century. It's a place to buy a quart of motor oil and enough snacks to tide a motorist over to his next destination.

The station, we are told, dates back to 1920. When it was sold to a new owner in the 1980s he was told, when applying for a new license, that the place did not exist. "Look again," the state worker was told. After a second check, the employee replied, "Oh! That's the one (station) that's been there forever."

It is good to see an independently-owned mom and pop station. Few remain. Most are company stations, the get-in-fast-leave-quick convenient one-stop operations run by employees waiting for their shifts to end.

* * *

Wooden fences extend along the road, enclosings estates near Upperville, the area noted for having some of the best horse farms in the country. Most of the horses are for fox hunting and pleasure, not for the pari-mutuel thoroughbred tracks of America. The farms become even larger en route to Middleburg, which is eight miles from Upperville.

Horse clubs, horse shows and fox hunts have been a tradition of the area since the 1840s, a tradition as old as the stone fences and plantations.

One of those plantation is Welborn. A historical marker notes that Welborn, a mile to the north, is an example of late 18th Century farm houses that evolved into an imposing mansion. It was at Welborn where F. Scott Fitzgerald and Thomas Clayton Wolfe stayed for a time in the 1930s. Each writer later published stories using the house as a setting."

Up ahead a marker reads: "At Atoka Rectors Crossroads on June 10, 1863, Company A, 43rd Battalion of Partisan Rangers, known as Mosby's Rangers, was formally organized."

John S. Mosby, for whom a section of U.S. 50 is named, was a civil war general whose independent cavalry unit conducted raids behind Union lines. This section of U.S. 50 is the John Mosby Highway, one of a number of other memorials for him we will note.

* * *

U.S. 50 becomes a four-lane highway for a short distance, then narrows to two lanes as it enters Middleburg, a town of 600 noted for its charm and distinguished visitors.

It was founded in 1787 by Leven Powell, a colonel in the Revolutionary War, who bought the land for $2.50 an acre from a cousin of George Washington.

The name Middleburg came from its central location between Alexandria and Winchester on the Ashby Gap trading route that eventually became U.S. 50. An overnight stop in those early days, it is a vacation destination today.

Middleburg is crowded with shops, crafts stores and assorted retail outlets to attract the casual visitor. "Relax! You're in the Village," reads a welcome amid the rustic old buildings.

Exterior view of Red Fox Tavern

A Safeway supermarket seems out of place, a 20th Century look in an 18th Century setting.

Middleburg is an attraction for visitors who come from throughout the nation to observe the fascination of the town, known as "the nation's horse and hunt capital."

The Red Fox Inn, a meeting location for John Mosby and his rangers, is called the oldest inn in America. It was at the Red Fox that Pierre Salinger, press secretary to President John F. Kennedy, sometimes conducted news conferences.

A marker in a garden type area across from the Red Fox notes: "This pavilion is dedicated (October 1995) to Jackie Kennedy Onassis and her happy years in the village."

The Windsor House Inn, dating back to 1824, was known as the Colonial Inn during the Civil War when meals were served to Union troops even though operators and employees were sympathetic to the cause of the South.

The John Mosby Restaurant is a busy stop at noon on a week day. The food is good, the attendants gracious, the atmosphere fitting for the history that surrounds it. It is a good place to capture the flavor of the town and to leaf through "Horse Country," identified as "the official publication of the Virginia Steeplechase Association."

It offers a glimpse of a lifestyle with which few Americans are familiar, a guide to urbane events such as the annual Virginia Foxhound Club show. A full page advertisement claims Horse Country Ltd. is the purveyor of the finest riding clothes. An insert in the magazine provides an opportunity for the wealthy to participate in the Irish Georgian Society raffle, a drawing limited to 150 chances at $1,000 a ticket.

This is not a magazine that caters to your $5-a-week-take-a-chance-on-a-state-lottery clientele.

That aside, the town of Middleburg is not a closed society. It is a place for Mr. Average American to spend some time, absorb history and hobnob with the more elite without feeling out of place.

And, for anyone who is impressed enough to want to stay, there is usually a magnificent estates for sale at $3 million and up.

* * *

U.S. 50 remains two lane as it passes horse and Angus cattle farms on its route to Aldie, five miles east of Middleburg. Aldie is the site of Aldie Mill, which dates back to the first decade of the 1800s and was the scene of a Civil War skirmish June 17, 1863.

From Aldie the road, now four lanes, turns southeast to Arcola en route to Chantilly. The Chantilly Battlefield, a short distance to the south of U.S. 50, was the site of fighting September 1, 1862, which left two Union generals dead.

* * *

Gone is country. Gone is leisurely motoring. The road no longer is for nature and history. It has become a destination, not an observation. Only cars, congestion and interchanges are ahead as we near metropolitan Washington.

U.S. 50 passes near Dulles International Airport and enters the Fairfax County suburbs, one after another. The road joins a multiplex with U.S. 29 in Fairfax City, eventually becoming a part of the six-lane Arlington Boulevard.

It skirts the northeast corner of Arlington National Cemetery, crosses the Potomac and eases its way down Constitution Avenue in Washington before joining U.S. 1 on its way northeast.

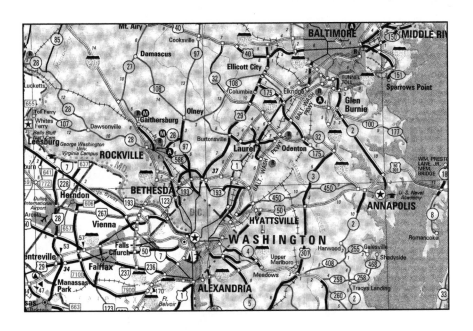

MARYLAND

U.S. 50 does not end in Washington. No longer, two-lane, it has miles to go before it reaches the Atlantic Ocean at Ocean City, Md. On its way, it will pass through Annapolis, the capital of Maryland and one of the nation's most striking and historic cities.

Most of the seaport city, site of the U.S. Naval Academy, can be seen on walking trips. Many of its structures date back 200 or more years, back almost to the time the city became the Maryland capital in 1695.

And it was the Statehouse here that served as the nation's capitol from 1783 to 1784.

* * *

U.S. 50 continues east from Annapolis, then crosses the Chesapeake Bay bridge, itself an engineering triumph. We have reached an end too Part I of our odyssey, leaving for another time our journey to the highway's terminus - or beginning in Ocean City.

We will return at another time to resume the journey along the road that passes through Queenstown before turning due south. At Cambridge it angles southeast to Salisbury, then continues east to Ocean City and the Atlantic Ocean.

PART II

Memories are - for each of us - the safety deposit boxes of our lives. Those each of us possess are ours alone. They belong to no other and none can take them from us.

Stretches of roads, frequently traveled, are etched in the recesses of our minds, certain locations reminding us of incidents of our past. A creek may remind us of the swimming hole of our youth. A spot along the road may recall an accident. A roadside park may revive thoughts of a joyful family picnic.

U.S. 50 is like that in Indiana for us for it is here that the road has been most frequently traveled. It is the section we know best.

QUOTABLE

"Are you here to pick persimmons?" - One of three men enjoying the fall scenery at the Medora Knobs overlook in Indiana.

———————

"Oh, we still use it three or four times a day." - An employee in the Martin County, Ind., clerk's office, commenting on an ancient spiral iron staircase leading to the second floor.

———————

"One of the areas where U.S. 50 is most essential is the Amish communities of Daviess County. " - Indiana Lt. Gov. Joe Kernan.

———————

"This has been a community that cares and that means a lot.
If a community doesn't care, it won't stay a community long." - A woman in Bridgeport, Ill.

———————

"When I was stationed in San Francisco, I would see those U.S. 50 signs and thank, man, my home is on that road." - A man at Carlyle, Ill.

———————

"We think he may have had too much to drink at sea." - A woman at the Mermaid House in Lebanon, Ill, explaining the name of the place given by a ship captain who claimed he had seen mermaids.

CHAPTER 7

INDIANA
WEST FROM SEYMOUR

Return with us now to Seymour where we begin our trip west toward St. Louis. We are back at U.S. 50 and Interstate 65, the intersection that makes Seymour the "Crossroads of Southern Indiana."

Indianapolis is 62 miles north, Louisville 55 miles south, Cincinnati 90 miles east, St. Louis 235 miles west.

Seymour today is a far different place than it was in 1820 when James Shields, the first settler, received a grant for Mule Crossing, the name he gave to the land he had homesteaded.

The farm, that prospered under Shield's son, Capt. Meedy Shields, was crossed by a north-south railroad in the 1840s. It became even more valuable when he volunteered to donate the right-of-way for an east-west railroad. The railroad accepted the offer . . . after it was agreed Seymour would be named after its engineer, J. Seymour, in a quid pro quo.

Befitting such negotiating ability, Shields entered politics and, as a state senator, persuaded the Indiana General Assembly to enact legislation requiring all trains to stop at railroad intersections. The action made Seymour a center where railroads exchanged freight and passengers.

By 1864, Mule Crossing had become a major crossing, its 1,553 residents incorporated as the town of Seymour.

* * *

It was an east-bound Ohio and Mississippi train that brought Seymour national attention in 1866 and made the Reno Gang the terrorists of railroads.

The gang, headed by brothers Frank, Simeon and William Reno, boarded the train east of Seymour, tossed the trainmen off, robbed the baggage car as it passed through Seymour and fled with $10,000.

Two years later, the Reno Gang robbed an express car south of Seymour of $96,000. Success bred greed and the gang extended its crime wave through five states.

Vigilantes eventually captured some of the men. A short time later three members of the gang were aboard a train headed to Brownstown for trial at the Jackson County Courthouse when vigilantes struck again. The three died on the end of ropes tied to limbs of a tree at the west edge of Seymour, an intersection that likely will forever be known as Hangman's Crossing.

* * *

U.S. 50 is four lane as it heads west from Interstate 65 at the east edge of Seymour. A giant Wal-Mart distribution center is at the southwest quadrant, one that dispatches semis, it seems, by the quarter-hour around the clock.

Once again business has followed the road, lined now with two fast food restaurants per acre instead for 150 bushels of corn. Discount stores, gasoline stations, motels, chain restaurants and strip malls extend for two miles, all seeking a share of the motorists' dollar.

Despite the growth to the east, downtown Seymour, population 15,700, looks unchanged over the years. As U.S. 50 eases its way through the old downtown area it passes Schneck Memorial, the Jackson County hospital, which takes our thoughts from the road.

* * *

[It was at Schneck where my dad died back in 1983, a few days short of his 95 birthday. He had seen the automobile when it was new, used horses and wagons to haul gravel to road sites, seen men fly, then walk on the moon. He had witnessed good

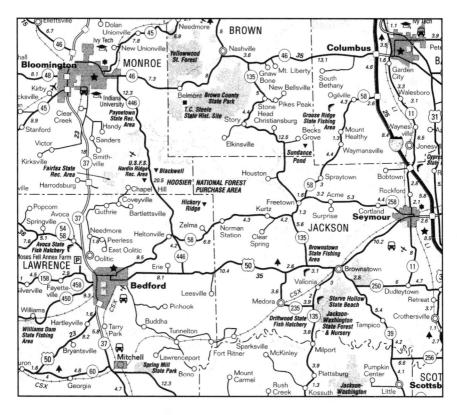

times and bad, war and peace, economic highs and lows and managed to endure hardships of the Great Depression. He had farmed, cut stone, driven a horse-drawn school hack, helped build a church and been a good neighbor. He was good at each of those things, but he was best at being a father.

[I can still hear my dad's laughter at an incident that had occurred three decades earlier across the street from the hospital. I was hitchhiking my way home from college when a neighbor stopped his westbound truck on U.S. 50, a smile as broad as the cab on his face.

["You don't know how happy I am to see you," he gushed. I wondered why until he swung his right thumb back toward his cargo, which was six tons of Happy Farmer fertilizer in 80-pound bags waiting to be unloaded. It was a time before trucks had mechanical equipment to unload cargo.

[We helped him unload the bags - one bag at a time - at a farm a few miles from home. "It's good to earn what you receive," my dad had laughed when he heard the story.

* * *

Off to the north from the road is Seymour High School, its gym seating 8,110 fans, an indication why the game of high school basketball is called Hoosier Hysteria.

Not far away to the south is the entrance to Freeman Field, a far different place in peace than in war. The base was activated in December, 1942, as a U.S. Army Air Force advanced training school for World War II twin-engine pilots. By war's end in 1945 the base, which included 413 structures and four 4,500-foot runways, had graduated more than 4,000 pilots.

The base, named for Indiana pilot Capt. Richard S. Freeman (1907-1940), was deactivated in 1948.

Within two years, some of its buildings were used to store surplus grain raised by area farmers in what was truly a "swords to plowshares" transition.

The base is now an industrial park and part of the air field is used as a municipal airport for charter and freight service.

* * *

Al's Heartbeat Cafe is at the west edge of Seymour, catering to diners and nostalgia fans. It is more than a cafe. It's also Al's "Fabulous 50s Museum."

The cafe is a place to return to the past, to a time of hand-dipped milkshakes, shiny chrome, neon lights and classic cars. Al is Al Skaggs, whose confessed love for classics Chevys, patriotism and nostalgia led him to choose U.S. 50 as a site for the restaurant in 1995.

Visitors can dine in booths or on stools at the counter. The food is not fabulous, but good, the atmosphere clean, the fixtures sparkling as were the 1950s.

An 1956 mint-conditioned Chevy pickup is in the restaurant section, a drive-in serving tray in the rolled down window. Music from the 50s rises from a juke box and drifts through the huge dining area. Among the countless fixtures are a full-size James

Dean cutout, a barber pole, gasoline pumps and antique Coca Cola signs.

A gift shop is open to diners. The museum admission is an added cost.

Motorists who travel the highway should stop in. After all - excuse the expression - it's only a heartbeat off the road.

* * *

Work is underway to rebuild sections of U.S. 50 west of Seymour. David Dye, project engineer for the State Highway Department, calls it a reconstruction project to add some left turn lanes. There are no plans, he says, to widen the road to four lanes.

U.S. 50 parallels the railroad west of Seymour for a distance as it passes through farm land and the Schneider Nursery, a huge outlet on both sides of the road for trees, shrubs and flowers.

The road rises over a hill to the west, the elevation providing a glimpse of rural Indiana back to the east. Not far to the north is the East Fork of White River, its sandy bottoms making the area prime land for watermelon production.

Some of those melons are on sale down the road toward Brownstown at Lubker's Farm Market, which a banner states is in its 75th year.

At the east edge of Brownstown, the road arcs to the south as it passes through the business district of the seat of Jackson County government.

* * *

Courthouse Square, the heart of Brownstown, is ringed by a wrought iron fence, the two-story buff brick Courthouse topped by a tower with a clock. The Courthouse has changed little over the years.

A historical marker on the U.S. 50 side of the square memorializes Col. John Ketcham (1782-1865) "fearless pioneer, ranger, surveyor, public servant, who dedicated this public square for seat of government of Jackson County when Brownstown was founded April 8, 1816."

A granite memorial to veterans of all wars is near the marker. In an opposite corner is a WWII tank, on which youngsters play, unaware of the horror of war.

Jackson County Courthouse at Brownstown

Across U.S. 50 from the courthouse are old store buildings, two and three stories, identified by engravings of names such as Fassold & Block and Wright-Vermilya. Most of the buildings remain occupied, at least on the lower level, for this is still a trading center for area residents. The Wal-Marts and Lowe's and other giants of retailing have yet to invade the quiet town.

Additional two-story buildings are on the north side of the square. One is occupied by Brownstown Feed & Supply, an old-type business reflecting the rural nature of the area around the town of 2,900.

The offices of the "Jackson County Banner," one of Indiana's great small town newspapers, are on the square's south side. The paper's twice-weekly editions still report tidbits, "items" some readers call then, from small hamlets throughout the county, personalizing the news which larger papers sometimes neglect to do.

An old livery stable off the square is the center for the Jackson County Historical Society. Its many mementos include relics of the days when horsepower came from horses not from giant farm tractors and high-speed cars.

One of Brownstown's major events is the Watermelon Festival, held each September as the community recognizes the importance of the cash crop to its economy.

Tourists, who are in the area in the fall when leaves turn into a myriad of colors, are advised to take a detour to Skyline Drive. The narrow three-mile paved road is a series of sharp turns, each turn a prelude to spectacular beauty. To the north is a postcard view of Brownstown, to the south a panorama of the Starved Hollow Lake area.

At their peak, the leaves become nature's masterpiece, a canvas of changing colors, a creation of nature too good to share, yet too good to keep from others.

* * *

Two blocks south of Courthouse Square, U.S. 50 turns from south to west, the road still two lanes. A few businesses, including an animal hospital, which translated means veterinary clinic, are along the route to its junction with Ind. 135.

A short distance to the south is a factory outlet store for Russell Stover Candies. It's a popular stop for the sweet tooth motorist.

* * *

U.S. 50 now extends west from Brownstown toward Bedford, a route that in 1935 replaced one that was much longer and more winding. The older route went south three miles to Vallonia, then west across the White River bottoms to Medora and on through Leesville to Bedford.

The new road, more than five miles shorter, opened September 25, 1935, to motorists who told the "Jackson County Banner" it was "the best and most beautiful section of road in the state."

It also was at that time one of the most expensive in the Indiana road system, the high cost or construction attributed to cuts through hills, steep inclines and long bridges.

* * *

On U.S. 50 west of the Ind. 135 junction, a grain elevator is to the north. The Marion-Kay Spices plant, its outlet open to visitors, is to the south.

A new bridge is under construction over White River a mile from Brownstown. A gravel excavation operation is to the south. Fields, large and fertile, but subject to the whims of the river after spring rains, are on both sides of the road.

The fields remain flat and sandy beyond the point where Ind. 135 turns north as it leaves its union with U.S. 50 and heads north toward Freetown.

A poultry operation is abandoned, a tombstone to the ever-changing trends of agriculture. To the rear, the hills rise over the Jackson-Washington State Forest.

* * *

[Ind. 235 connects Medora to the south with U.S. 50, an intersection called Medora Junction. The location awakens another memory.

[Four decades ago, in 1950 as we recall, we again were hitchhiking home, this time with a friend. We had stood at the junction an hour or more, our thumbs pointing from tired arms. A ride seemed hopeless.

[From Brownstown came a familiar looking car. "We're in luck," I said, "That's my dad's car."

[Dad glanced to the right, waved, being a friendly person who knew no strangers, and drove on without reducing speed.

[We arrived home an hour or more later. "Thanks a lot!" we tell him. He confesses: "I thought that looked like you, but you said you weren't coming home this weekend, so I just kept driving." It was a story the three of us would recall with laughter for years to come.]

* * *

A store and service station that once was at the southeast corner of Medora Junction no longer exists. The Midway Apostolic Church is nearby. A trucking firm is to the west at the base of the Medora Knobs.

The Medora Knobs rise to the west, U.S. 50 slicing through deep cuts as it makes its way west. There is no passing lane and cars slow behind loaded trucks that down shift to lower gears to make the incline.

In the money-tight depression of the 1930s, and later in World War II when gasoline was rationed, motorists sometimes turned off the engines of their cars and coasted down the knobs, the inertia taking them past Medora Junction into the White River bottoms.

We turn off U.S. 50 to the north and drive into the Medora Knobs Overlook past a sign that advises visitors that there are no restroom facilities in the park. Three men are under the roof in the open shelter house, sipping beer and enjoying each other's company as they relax near the bluff formed by the road cut.

They are there, they say, to escape the people in Brown County, a county to the north which is a favorite of tourists each fall when leaves are in full color.

"You here to pick persimmons?" one asks, nodding toward some persimmon trees.

"Just enjoying the scenery," we tell him. The view back to the east is a marvel of the Maker's creation, the color as expansive as that of the crowded Brown County the men have escaped.

"Good place to do it," the man replies, expressing fear the park may be eliminated if plans to improve the road become reality. A check later with the Indiana Department of Transportation reveals no such work is planned along the route until at least 2006.

An old pump, the kind once used to draw water from the depths of the earth, remains among the hardwood - and persimmon - trees. We leave the men to enjoy the day, the persimmons we leave for others to gather.

A "Coon Hunt" sign, a short distance west, points north at at Jackson County Road 790 West. Raccoon hunting is a big sport in this area of southern Indiana, so big that some hunters are accused of caring more about their coon dogs than their wives. It is a sport that existed long before the arrival of animal rights activisits.

To the south a gasoline station, identified as "Bob's Service," is closed. Stations have come and gone - more going than coming - in the 65 years U.S. 50 has followed this route. An old house, buffered from the north winds by a row of cedar trees, is to the west. It has been a fixture ever since the road opened.

Rumpke of Indiana, a sanitary landfill, is off to the south on a hill overlooking the headwaters of Guthrie Creek. It is another monument to America's waste.

A building to the south is a reminder of the late 1940s when it housed a store, which was a place for farmers to stop for soft drinks and snacks when delivering grain to Medora and Brownstown.

At Clearspring Road a sign promotes the "Harvest Festival" in the town of Clearspring three miles to the north. Autumn brings more fall festivals than persimmons to Indiana.

U.S. 50 in this area winds through woods and small fields for this area is not prime farm land.

* * *

The past reawakens as we reach what is known as Shady Springs. It is not the Shady Springs we knew in our youth. Back then it was a roadhouse, the infamous roadhouse, some folks called it.

Born in prohibition, it remained a night spot long after liquor again became legal. It was a place couples could bring their own booze, order set ups (Cokes and ice), drink, dance and wile away Friday and Saturday nights. It also was a place for youths in their mid-teens to observe life as lived by their more worldly elders.

Shady Springs lost its glitter when men left to fight World War II and women took jobs in defense plants. The world had turned more serious. In a dramatic switch, the grounds became the Shady Spring Tabernacle, a religious center. It is now the Shady Springs Campgrounds.

Not far to the west, Fleshman's Pit Stop, once a restaurant and convenience store, is now closed, another indicator of the uncertainties of entrepreneurship.

Down the road is Larry's Country Roadhouse, "fine dining and entertainment," a sign says. Larry is Larry Rollins, a singer of some fame. It still is a place to dine, but it is not like the roadhouse of the Depression years. There is no dancing, no drinking and no longer entertainment as there was in the mid-1990s when musicians came on weekends to play and sing songs like

"Faded Love," "Thirty Acres of Bottom Land," "Long Black Veil" and "You Are My Flower."

Rollins, in his younger years, sang the title song in John Mellencamp's movie, "Falling From Grace," and cut his own records and performed at the Little Nashville (Indiana) Opry.

LAWRENCE COUNTY

The Lawrence County line is just to the west of Larry's Roadhouse. An old combine rusts off the north side of road, another burial site for unused equipment.

Two miles to the south is Leesville, which was on U. S. 50 before the road was relocated. Leesville is one of the area's oldest town, first settled in 1810. Three years later it was the site of a Potawatomi Indian massacre.

The first school in Lawrence County opened at Leesville in 1813, the first high school in 1858. The students are now bused elsewhere, but a school remains, well maintained as a civic center by the civic minded.

* * *

Back on U.S. 50 we pass Ern Speer's old place, now a church retreat. Ern, a big man himself, was a middle man when it came to produce.

Ern toured area farms in his pick up truck, collecting cream, butter and eggs for sale to produce firms, keeping a small fee for his service. Now farmers, like city dwellers, buy their cream, eggs and butter at supermarkets.

Ern has gone to his reward, like the men and women who shared his life. His property is now a religious retreat called Camp Challenge.

U.S. 50 crosses Back Creek, once the site of swimming holes for the areas young. Three miles up Back Creek Road, sometimes called Possum Holler, but officially County Road 950 East, is the place of our youth. The road is paved now, the route over the steep hills wider, the memories deeper.

U.S. 50 ascends the hill to the west, then becomes almost as straight as an arrow. It will remain that way for the next six miles.

The Plaza Motel is open but most of its rooms are now occupied by more permanent tenants. A water tower is along the road, a part of a rural water system that has opened the area, where wells often failed, to development.

The Farmers Market, a new convenience stop for motorists, is at the Ind. 446 junction with U.S. 50. Ind. 446, a scenic drive, crosses the causeway at Lake Monroe, Indiana's largest body of water, as it links the area with Bloomington.

Not far away is the site of what once were Jack Browns' Fairview Cabins, an overnight stop for tourists who could choose from a number of the small units. The office was in a store, which was a convenient place for neighbors to pick up groceries and other items they had forgotten on trips to nearby towns.

Occasional slot machines seen in the place at times taught teen-agers the perils of gambling.

To the west a half mile was Woodland Retreat, a roadhouse and "tourist camp."

Tourists cabins, many of them mom and pop businesses, have disappeared from roadsides, replaced by clusters of motels at major interchanges.

[It is this area of U.S. 50 that stirs one of our earliest memories. It was here we came as a five-year-old in 1934 to watch the road bed built. We recall men, the reins of their teams of horses around their necks, holding wide their arms to grasp the handles of slips that scooped dirt for the traffic lanes. It was a time when manpower was cheaper than machines, a time of depression when thoughtful contractors hired men whose horses helped them earn a living.]

Maple Leaf, another tourist cabin operation, was further west at the Shawswick-Heltonville intersection. It also was a roadhouse, a place to bring a bottle of booze, dance and forget the financial woes of a difficult era. Tourist cabins were to the north and east.

The late Jim Guthrie, a Lawrence County historian, related this conversation, likely apocryphal and - as far as we know - not necessarily related to Maple Leaf:

Tourist: "How much are your rooms for the night?"

Tourist cabin operator: "I don't know. No one has ever rented one for a full night."

* * *

Small housing developments are on the south side of U.S. 50. To the north is a garden center, not far from where the road turns to the southwest toward Bedford. A convenience store remains nearby, a fixture for almost half a century.

Off to the north is an old drive-in theater, like tourist cabins a thing of the past. A steel fabricating factory is now on the site.

In the distance is Bedford-North Lawrence High School a consolidation of Bedford and seven county high schools. It was a hotbed of basketball in the late 1980s when legend Damon Bailey led the Stars to the 1990 state championship and broke the state's individual scoring record along the way.

On the approach into Bedford, U.S. 50 passes Otis Park, the site of one of Indiana's better golf courses. A bandstand and stone fences, creations of the Works Progress Administration in the Great Depression, remain in the park, which was given to the city by newspaper publisher Fred Otis in the 1930s.

From the park, U.S. 50 turns west and ascends a hill into the Bedford, "Stone City," it is called, the county seat of Lawrence County, which is "home of astronauts," tourism directors proclaim. Three U.S. astronauts, Vigil "Gus" Grissom, one of the original seven, and Ken Bowersox and Charles Walker, grew up in the county.

The Bedford Chamber of Commerce has linked the limestone and the astronauts for its motto: "Soar Into the Future from a Rock Solid Foundation."

* * *

Had there been no mosquitoes there may not have been a Bedford. The county seat was to have been at Palestine, a settlement near White River to the south. That changed, however, when mosquitoes at the site became so bad the community packed up and moved north in 1825 to what would become Bedford, the name coming from Bedford County, Tenn.

* * *

At H street in Bedford, U.S. 50 is divided for about six blocks, the westbound route turning north at H Street for one block where it becomes part of 15th Street. The eastbound lane uses 16th Street.

Between the two routes is the Lawrence County Courthouse, limestone, of course, which looks much the same as when it was dedicated on Armistice Day in 1930.

[In the eyes of a child of the 1930s, the Courthouse looked like the world's largest building. It seemed spacious inside, the marble floors and steps far more elegant than the wooden floors at school. It was a place for men to gather on Saturdays and swap stories while their wives shopped.

[As years passed and we grew older, the size of the courthouse seemed to diminish, but the memories of visits to the offices inside never faded.]

The square is far different place now, however, than it was on Saturday nights at mid-century when every parking space was filled, stores were open and fans sought relief from the heat in the air-conditioned Indiana and VonRitz theaters. There now are no crowds on the square, no downtown theater. The crowds are at home, viewing videos, at a theater complex at the edge of town or finding pleasures elsewhere. It is much the same at other cities where we have stopped on U.S. 50.

Off the square on the northeast corner, is the vacant reminder of the Greystone Hotel, one of the state great hotels of the 1930s and 1940s. It fell into disrepair, its clientele having preferred cheaper, less elegant, surroundings, then was razed in the early 1990s.

A few feet away is the Masonic Temple, one of the city's landmark. It was in the temple's basement that John Katis' pool parlor was located, the hangout where many teens of the 1940s and 1950s learned to shoot pool and billiards.

Bedford's population, estimated at 14,000 has changed little over the years. Its business area has, however. Businesses that once clustered around the square, now line 16th Street to the west, leaving the heart of the city to law firms, banks, offices and small stores.

Area limestone, extricated from nearby quarries and cut and shaped at mills, has been used to help build some of America's great structures. The stone can be found in the Empire State Building in New York City, the Chicago Museum of Fine Arts, the Mellon Institute in Pittsburgh and the Washington Cathedral and a number of government buildings in Washington.

A museum called "Land of Limestone" is open at the Bedford branch of Oakland City University, which is north of the square on I Street. It is an exhibit which chronicles the varied uses of limestone and pays tribute to its place in the city's history.

Limestone is still quarried and milled, but its role as an employer is now shared with General Motors, Ford and other industries.

U.S. 50 reunites at M Street where it makes a 90-degree turn south. Two blocks south and to the east is Green Hill Cemetery, noted for its elaborately carved tombstones, fashioned from limestone.

* * *

The road swings to the southwest over a four-lane section, relocated four decades ago from a more congested route, passing a restaurant or two and other businesses. It merges with Ind. 37, crosses White River, and passes a small business center devastated by a tornado in 1990. Evidence of the destruction can still be seen near the intersection, where U.S. 50 turns west at a stoplight, leaving Ind. 37 to continue its route south to Mitchell and beyond.

* * *

In 1919, U.S. 50 - then known as State Roads 4 and 41 - was taken into the federal system. The stretch from Lawrence County to Shoals was surfaced with bitumen in 1928, then partially paved with concrete in 1933.

Before then, the road went south to Mitchell before going west toward Shoals and Loogootee. What was to be U.S. 50 opened in the early 1930s, shortening the distance to those Martin County towns.

By then cars were becoming a necessity rather than a luxury. The Indiana Automobile Regulations Act of 1925 established uniform speed limits and rules of the road. The state required a driver's license for the first time in 1929, when it enacted other traffic regulations.

* * *

The road west from Ind. 37 passes the Lawrence County Fairgrounds not far from a road that leads to the north to Bluesprings Cavern, an awesome creation of nature in this area of underground caves.

A one-hour guided tour in a lighted electric boat extends through narrow underground passages formed by what is called "Myst'ry" River that runs deep in the hills. Crawfish and blind fish are visible in the light as the boat eases through a network of limestone caves. Stalactites and rock formations appear along the steep canyon walls.

The cost is reasonable, but the tours are conducted only from April through October. Spouses or others who disdain caves can relax in the gift shop and read about what is being missed.

If the Bluesprings Cavern had been a tourist attraction in the 1930s and 1940s, visitors could have stayed at the Whip-Poor-Will. The tourist cabins, called by some as the best of any around, were opened by Lincoln "Curly" Dunbar, a former Lawrence County sheriff. The motel, like others along the route, closed sometime around mid-century.

Not far away is the site of what was once the St.-Cinn Motel, so called because of its equidistance from St. Louis to the west, Cincinnati to the east. It, too, is gone. So is what was once Ed Hirsch's Ghost Town, a museum/general store of sorts that had among other things a jail cell.

The area to the west is rolling, the land better suited for grazing than for corn and soybeans. Bryantsville, a small hamlet with a church and a radio station transmitter, is near the road as it runs southwest.

Beyond the Ind. 60 intersection is the town of Huron, which was platted as Hoard's Station as a tribute to pioneer landowner William Hoard. Settlers who had arrived by 1855 renamed it for Huron County, Ohio, from which they had moved.

It is another town on U.S. 50 that grew up along the east-west railroad which became the B&O and is now part of the CSX system.

Huron, like other small communities, lost much of its vigor and part of its heart when the high school closed in 1963 and its students were sent to Mitchell. The school, later a Head Start center, is now privately owned, its occupants an antique and gift shop and fitness center.

A filling station remains, so does the post office, but the general store/restaurant no longer is in business. Other than a small steel fabrication factory, there is no industry. Native sandstone, shaped in blocks and mounted on skids, is for sale just west of town.

* * *

[Time is relative. A minute to a child is an hour. An hour for a senior citizen is a minute. Huron is 23 miles from Heltonville but those bus rides to Huron for basketball games in the 1940s seemed much longer. The distance today seems no longer than a cruise around the block.]

MARTIN COUNTY

Martin County has been noted for decades for having fewer people and less financial wealth than most counties of the state. As author/historian Harry Holt noted, it is, however, rich in romance, tradition, tragedy and scenic beauty.

The county is long and narrow, just 12 miles across from east to west, the route U.S. 50 takes.

The entire county has 10,400 residents, more than 35 percent of which live in Shoals and Loogootee, the two major communities.

* * *

A Lion's Club sign at the entrance to Martin County from the east, promotes the Catfish Festival, an annual July event at Shoals, as well as the beauty of the counties hills.

Semi traffic in the area is heavy, this being the major east-west route between Interstates 70 and 64. The trucks, however, do not detract from the view as the road circles a hill, the hardwood trees to the side a vista of color. U.S. 50 is an ideal drive in the autumn, the traffic less heavy than in more publicized areas.

* * *

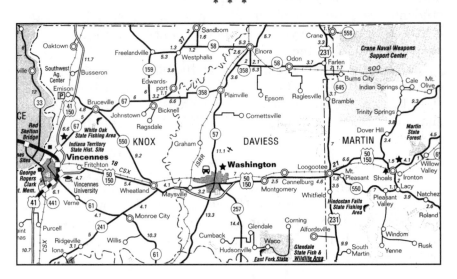

U.S. 50 tops a long incline where Ind. 650 leads to the south. The entrance to Martin County State Forest is to the north.

Ind. 650 is less than a mile long, built to connect the U.S Gypsum Company to U.S. 50. It is one of two gypsum plants in the county, the other National Gypsum, which we will see to the south of U.S. 50 en route into Shoals.

Gypsum is a white mineral used in the manufacture of plaster of Paris and in Portland cement, wallboards and fertilizers. Its discovery, according to a 1958 edition of the "Indianapolis Star," was "the fulfillment of a dream of dramatic wealth, but also the promise of a fabulous future for the hard pressed citizenry." The claim would be an exaggeration even though the two plants added to the county's tax base and brought jobs that would not otherwise have been available.

The Martin County State Forest is a 7,023-acre preserve of rugged hills, deep woods and long hiking trails. Much of the original work on roads and trails was done by the Civilian Conservation Corps in 1933-34.

* * *

U.S. 50 enters Shoals from the northeast past Shoals Community High School, whose athletic teams are known as the Jug Rox, a name that will become apparent shortly. A softball complex is in a valley at the east edge of town.

The R & J Food Mart is at the southwest corner of the intersection where U.S. 150 from the southeast joins U.S. 50 which it will accompany to Vincennes. Chances are those who stop at R & J on weekend mornings will find men with time on their hands and doughnuts and laughter on their minds. The conversations will be lively, but friendly.

Just to the west is Bo-Mac's, an old-type drive-in, one where a waitress arrives at the window as soon as the car is parked. A few tables are outside for diners on warm days. "We serve genuine roasted chicken - stop in for an after school snack," invites a sign.

* * *

[Just to the west our mind reverts back to a September day in 1951. We are on one of seven chartered Greyhound buses bound from Fort Custer, Mich., to Camp Breckenridge, Ky. A bus station, which no longer is here, was an oasis for the 400 Army recruits aboard. The restrooms were as welcome as the snacks that were available.]

* * *

This Martin County seat of 850 residents hasn't always been Shoals. It began as Natchez, became Pleasant Valley and was known as Halbert's Bluff before being renamed Shoals in 1868.

Buildings on north-south Main Street, despite improvements, look much as they did in the 1950s, still an idyll of rural America. Velma's Diner remains a place where folks meet to eat and exchange news in modest surroundings.

Shoppers browse through the Alco Dime Store, much like the five-and-dime outlets of mid-century. It is packed with merchandise equal to a Wal-Mart which has yet to invade the county. It is good to see a town whose businesses remain mom and pop operations.

Martin County Courthouse at Shoals

A mural that extends for what looks like 100 feet is on the side of Alco Store facing U.S. 50. It promotes the Catfish Festival, portrays the Jug Rock, pictures a cut through a bluff on U.S. 50, a river bend and Hindostan Falls. "Boating, scenic drives, fishing, hunting, camping, hiking, genealogy and history," notes the mural made possible by the Catfish Festival, Alco Dime Store and the Martin County Chamber of Commerce.

Shoals is divided by the East Fork of White River, which has flooded a number of times, the most severe devastation in 1913 and 1937. The spanning of the river by U.S. 50 in 1932 brought one of Shoals great celebrations. Decorated elaborately, the bridge was floodlighted while residents danced to two orchestras amid a crowd so dense no one could walk across the span. That bridge has been replaced, but the event remains a part of Shoals' history and a pleasant memory for those left to remember the occasion.

A street angles off U.S. 50 west of the bridge to the 130-year-old Martin County Courthouse, a modest two-story brick painted gray. Unlike most county courthouses, this one is not in an old shopping district. Its square has no businesses, no law offices, no banks.

A circular iron stairway leads from the clerk's office on the first floor to the judge's chambers on the second level. Installed before the days of elevators, it still is in use, "three or four times a day," says an employee.

A memorial to all veterans is out front on the lawn dotted with trees that appear as old as the courthouse. Across a street is the Martin County Senior Citizens Center. The Martin County jail is on the opposite side of the courthouse.

* * *

U.S. 50 rises from the river valley to ascend a hill to the west. It is midway up the hill that we find the Jug Rock, one of Shoals' most notable landmarks, almost hidden in the summer by the trees that surround it.

It is in a depression of sorts, approachable by narrow paths, maybe 100 feet from the roadside. No signs point to the rock that is near what was once Pinnacle Park, now a residential area. The only parking is at a short, narrow pull off at the edge of U.S. 50.

Formed by erosion of the sandstone around it, the "Jug" is 42 to 60 feet tall, depending on the source. It is 20 feet in diameter, topped by a flat surface called the stopper by some. Vines and other growth have found life in the dirt on the top.

A history of Shoals describes the Jug Rock, which led Shoals High School athletes to be known as the "Jug Rox," a more memorable title than Bears, Cubs, Lions, Tigers and Panthers:

"The picturesque residuum is the remaining core created by weathering of the massive sandstone ledge forming the pinnacle. Since the pillar stands alone without any adjacent ledge, it is one of the mystifying stand rocks in the U.S."

Another writer describes it as "a fantastically eroded sandstone oddity." And another calls the jug shaped mass "a giant sentinel without any apparent cliff to indicate its creation."

No matter, how it is described, it is a Shoals landmark, one no other small town can claim.

* * *

Sign at west entrance to town of Shoals

At the Shoals Overlook near the top of the hill, James Holt is resting after his morning walk. He talks about the Jug Rox, says he thinks it was formed by a glacier, but admits he is not an authority on it.

"I just know it is there. I don't know how many hundred years it has been there."

Holt is a Shoals native. "I've lived here all my life," he says, "except when I was in service for sixteen years, nine months and twenty-eight days."

The overlook is high on a bluff far above a horseshoe bend in White River to the south. It is a quiet place, despite the occasional stress of westbound trucks lumbering up the hill.

The small park, like the mural back on the Alco Store, is a community project. Benches are marked with donors such as the

Martin County Tourism Association, the Historical Society, Shoals Jaycees and Tri Kappa Sorority.

We linger a while, enjoying the conversation with James Holt.

"Have a safe trip," he tells us as we walk to the car. Hoosiers care for others, even those they've never seen before and likely won't meet again.

The Hoosier Hills tourist cabins that once were near the overlook at U.S. 50 and Ind. 450 are gone. So is the Ridge View gas station. God's creations like the Jug Rock remain for centuries. The business and structures men make are of much shorter duration.

* * *

Construction of U.S. 50 through the area remains a tribute to its designers, engineers and builders back in the early 1930s. A grade, two miles west of Shoals, required an open cut 100 feet deep through solid sandstone for 500 feet. Rock slides on each side caused it to be 300 feet wide when finished.

The excavation, known as Peek's Cut because it went through a farm owned by the Peek family, was the deepest in Indiana at the time. It was first thought a tunnel could be cut through the grade, but the solid rock made that impossible.

* * *

Trucks account for much of the traffic on this day between Shoals and Loogootee, but occasional passing lanes make driving easier on steep inclines. A few farms are in a valley between the hills. Some houses are on a ridge above the road. A northern bend brings White River to a point near the highway.

A sign at the east edge of Loogootee points the way to Hindostan Falls, a series of three-to-four foot falls across the river.

* * * *

Loogootee, population 2,900, is Martin County's only city, a city being a community with a mayor and council. It is "Low-go-tee," not "Log-a-tee" or various other pronunciation sometimes used by radio and television sportscasters reading scores of the high school basketball games.

And it is basketball that has helped make Loogootee a familiar name in Indiana, at least to sports fans. A sign on the water tower is a tribute to the town's Loogootee High School Lions teams: State Final Four in 1970, state runners up in 1975 when the Lions lost to Marion in the state finals. Those were years before class basketball, back when Loogootee was "the people's choice" against much bigger schools.

The water tower also recognizes player Jim Trout, the 1970 winner of the Trester Award, the tournament's top individual prize. Not mentioned is Jack Butcher, the coach of the Lions for 40 years who is or will be (there being some conflict in records), the winningest coach in state basketball history. His teams have won more than 750 games.

Loogootee, founded by Thomas N. Goatee, a descendant of French ancestors, was platted in 1853. It prospered when the Ohio and Mississippi Railroad (later called the B&O) arrived a few years later, opening the way to the east and west.

The railroad's significance has declined. Much of the city's's commerce and trade is now dependent on trucks that arrive and leave on U.S. 50 and U.S. 231.

Buildings in downtown Loogootee, north of U.S. 50 along U.S. 231, look much as they did in pictures from the mid-1950s. The businesses, though, have changed. Like all towns, many of the stores have moved out along U.S. 50 where more parking is available.

Stopping places for motorists also have changed over the year. Gone, for example, is Vincent Arvin's Standard Oil Station at the intersection of the two roads.

The centers of activity at mid-morning are a Dairy Queen and a Hardee's. Both are busy, the customers mostly local residents. A waitress at the Dairy Queen insists an out of-town visitor accept a senior citizen card - "10 percent off" - just in case he comes to town again. Folks in small towns know the value of money.

A section of U.S. 50, joined for a few blocks by U.S. 231, is four lane. A Beuhler's Buy Low grocery and pharmacy is along the route. Across the way is the Wonder Inn restaurant and lounge.

The road narrows to four lanes at a curve where U.S. 231 turns south toward Jasper. U.S. 50 resumes its route west, passing the impressive Loogootee City Park and a modern nursing home complex. Montgomery is seven miles away, Washington fourteen.

DAVIESS COUNTY

U.S. 50 is lined by farms and soybean and corn fields as it enters Daviess (pronounced Davis) County from the east. It is a county rich in natural resources, oil, coal and fertile farm land. The road is two lane, straight, unwavering as it heads toward Montgomery.

It was in this area that what would become U.S. 50 was built around 1915. A newspaper picture from that year shows wagons, pulled by teams of horses and mules driven by farmers, waiting for work to start on the gravel road.

To the north is the small town of Cannelburg. A factory which makes wooden trusses for building is at the side of the road. A big turkey farm is nearby.

Traffic slows to 10 mph behind a giant farm machine. It is a Monday morning, the start of a new week, but motorists seem patient for there are no horn blasts or angry words. Farming, like coal and oil, is a big part of the county's economy, a fact not lost on drivers backed up behind the farm machinery.

* * *

A sign at the edge of Montgomery notes the town is the "home of the annual Turkey Trot Festival - second weekend in September. Sponsored by the Montgomery Ruritan Club." The area is a center of turkey production and a reason to trot out the importance of the feathered fowl to the town.

A service station and a business or two are on U.S. 50. The town is to the north, the Gasthof, an Amish restaurant and gift center, beyond that.

St. Peter's Catholic Church is on the highest rise in town, its spires visible for miles across the county's flat terrain. The parish

St. Peter's Catholic Church in Montgomery

was formed in 1818 as the area's second oldest, a plaque notes, and adds: "Father Bartholomew Piers designed the present Gothic style church by carving a perfect miniature model with a pen knife. St. Peter's was consecrated July 18, 1869, at a cost of $8,000. Father Piers served as pastor for 48 years until his death in 1895."

An antique mall nearby is decorated with a mural of assorted colors - blue, yellow, pink, orange, red and black - accented by a picture of an Amish wagon and buggy. A big grain elevator operation is nearby.

Not far from the church is Barr-Reeve High School, a consolidation of Montgomery, Barr Township and Alfordsville.

* * *

U.S. 50 turns slightly to the southwest from Montgomery. Big farms are to the south, the Country Oaks Golf Club to the north.

To the west is the Amish Kountry Korner, neatly packed with assorted cheeses, cured hams, jellies, candies, snacks, quilts, crafts and antiques. It is an outlet more for travelers than the dozens of Amish families who live on nearby farms. Amish furniture is for sale in a building next door.

The number of Amish in the county is uncertain, but the total is significant. Amish farms are numerous to the north of U.S. 50, a highway Indiana Lt. Gov. Joseph E. Kernan calls important to small communities in southern Indiana. "The road," he says, "is essential to commerce and industry. One of the areas it is most evident is through the Amish communities of Daviess County."

Beyond, huge billboards along the road detract from the view to the north and south. A sign notes an Ostrich Ranch off the road, ostriches being a relatively new enterprise for farmers. Gone, however, is an old drive-in theater, a victim of television and rental movies.

* * *

Traffic on U.S. 50 through the city of Washington, population 11,000, was diverted in the early 1990s. A bypass now circles south around the city, a route that intersects with Ind. 57 and Ind. 257 on its way to the west.

The old road through town is now called the National Highway. The diversion of traffic does not appear to have detracted from businesses. Old U.S. 50 is the site of motels, fast food restaurants, a Wal-Mart store and a shopping complex, all of which indicate the town is growing east from downtown.

* * *

Washington had its origin as Liverpool, a town platted in 1815. The plat for the town of Washington was recorded two years later, merging the Liverpool lots. Washington existed as a town until 1867 when citizens, unhappy with municipal authorities, voted to dissolve the Town Board, a newspaper reporting:

"Our citizens have tried the beauties of a corporation for some time and have found, to their sorrow, that it was impossible to find men for the various offices who would see the law strictly enforced."

The absence of government was as bad as its presence, leading to the creation of a city form of government in 1871.

Washington, the Daviess County seat, grew up around the east-west Ohio & Mississippi (later the B&O) which arrived in 1857, joining the stage coach as the town's only modes of outside transportation. The railroad, a historian noted, "awakened Washington and the surrounding county to real life. New men and fresh capital came in and the first real boom that Washington had long hoped for began to be a realization."

Much of the city's history remains in the old B&O Railroad Depot, now home to the Daviess County Chamber of Commerce, Visitors Bureau and the Daviess County Growth Council.

A marker notes that the Mission Revival style depot was built in 1906 and restored in 1990 as part of Washington's commercial historic district. The depot was the only stop made in Indiana when President Dwight D. Eisenhower's funeral train passed through the state April 1, 1969.

Like Loogootee, part of Washington's fame throughout the state stems from basketball. Its Hatchet teams won state championships in 1930, 1941 and 1942. Its girls teams have had more success in recent years, rated high in state polls. The high school gym has 7,090 seats, enough for almost 70 percent of the city's population.

Main Street, which is north of the old U.S. 50 route, remains much as it has for decades. Unlike other towns, businesses still occupy most of the storefronts and some outlets report the removal of traffic on the bypass has increased business because the area is now less congested.

Another shopping complex, a strip mall with a grocery and a variety of other businesses, is at the west edge of the city on the old route.

North-south Ind. 57 links old U.S. 50 to the bypass, the Black Buggy restaurant and bakery on the connector route. It is Saturday morning and the Amish establishment is packed as diners take advantage of the buffet - "$4.25, coffee included." The buffet choices are extensive, the bakery items varied; attendants are cordial, the decor bright. Most of the customers are local folks, who likely dine there often.

The Black Buggy, however, is more than a restaurant-bakery. It is complex that includes the Black Beauty General Store, Victorian Lace Country Ruffles, a produce and deli outlet and an open flea market.

To the south, a new motel, a restaurant and a fast food outlet are at the northeast quadrant of the U.S. 50 bypass and Ind. 57 crossing. If an intersection opens, anywhere it seems, motels and fast food outlets will follow.

Back on the bypass headed west, we spot the skeleton of a giant industrial complex rising off to the south on Maysville Road. We will learn later from David R. Cox, executive director of the Daviess County Growth Council, it is the site of a $270 million Grain Processing Corporation facility. The operation is expected to employ 150 workers and process 500 acres of No. 2 yellow corn daily.

GPC, we are told, is a processor of food, pharmaceutical and industrial products.

* * *

KNOX COUNTY

The west fork of White River divides Daviess and Knox, Indiana's first county.

Giant electric transmission lines run north from a power plant to the south on White River. Work is underway to complete widening U.S. 50 to four lane from the Washington bypass to beyond the Wabash River. Giant earthmovers, resembling dinosaurs, are at the roadside as we enter the town of Wheatland.

Like other small towns, Wheatland, too, has seen better days, even though a service station, motel, grain elevator and a grocery remain. If there is a restaurant in town, we do not find it. Gone is the old Wheatland High School, its one time Jeeps having joined with other schools to become the Spartans of South Knox.

From Wheatland, U.S. 50 follows a straight line west, paralleling the CSX Railroad. Cattle graze on pastures, the grass freshened by the morning dew.

* * *

Fritchton, no longer on U.S. 50, was left behind and isolated from traffic when the highway was rerouted to the south as a four-lane road east from Vincennes.

It is another town both time and traffic have passed. Its high school also is gone, now part of the South Knox consolidation. A sign near the Palmyra Township Volunteer Fire Department notes that the site was once the "Home of the Fritchton Eagles."

The Eagles basketball teams were the pride of the town, a focus of community pride. Among its former coaches was the late John Baratto, who later would lead East Chicago Washington to the 1960 state title. In Indiana, towns are known by their basketball teams.

Like other towns, the loss of the school took away Fritchton's sense of community and robbed it of its cohesiveness. There are no meeting places for residents to gather, the only businesses a Knox County Water office and a GTE telephone building.

We cancel our plans to capture the flavor of the town over coffee. There no longer are restaurants in Fritchton.

* * *

Back on U.S. 50 our eyes are drawn back to the eastern horizon. God has awakened the world to rise another day. The air is cooler than the earth, the sun, peeking its head from its night cover, creating a brilliance through the fog that arises from streams and creeks over unharvested fields of corn and soybeans. The crops promise a good yields to come, the land is clean, the sky pure, the air free from pollution. All is well, despite warnings from skeptics on Saturday morning talk shows of holes in the ozone and the shedding of tears over global warming.

* * *

U.S. 50 splits at the east edge of Vincennes, the four-lane route joining north-south U.S. 41 for a short distance before turning west as it crosses the Wabash River over the Red Skelton bridge into Illinois. Skelton, the late comedian, was a Vincennes native.

Old U.S. 50 continues as a business route into the heart of historic Vincennes, Indiana's oldest city.

* * *

Vincennes is not a drive-through-pickup-history city. It is one to observe at leisure for there is much to see and much to learn. The river Wabash is one of song; the city Vincennes one of novels. Landmarks note the city's role in the development of the nation.

It was here the French established an outpost and fur trading center around 1700. In 1732 it was fortified by a French-Canadian explorer with the noble sounding name of Francois Marie Bissot, Sieur de Vincennes. The settlement was ceded to the British in 1763 and was known as Fort Sackville when seized by U.S. forces led by Gen. George Rogers Clark in 1779.

It was here where Vincennes University became the first land grant college in the Northwest Territory in 1801. The university remains as does Grouseland, the home of former William Henry Harrison when he was governor of the old Indiana Territory. Open most of the year to tourists, also, is the birthplace of Maurice Thompson, author of "Alice of Old Vincennes," a novel set during the Revolutionary War.

Still here are the territorial capitol, the Old Cathedral and the French Cemetery. A replica of the Western Sun print shop remains near the old capitol. The newspaper, started in 1804 as the Indiana Gazette, later became the "Western Sun" and in a merger in 1931 became the "Vincennes Sun-Commercial," which still serves the area. The publisher of the Sun-Commercial is Michael Quayle, brother of former Vice President Dan Quayle.

On the banks of the Wabash is the George Rogers Clark National Historical Park. It is a tribute to Clark and his unit of 170 men who made an arduous and courageous 18-day trek from Kaskaskia to recapture the strategic fort. It was a victory that would eventually force the British to cede to the U.S. an area that includes Ohio, Indiana, Illinois, Michigan, Wisconsin and part of Minnesota.

The granite and marble memorial, rounded and fronted with columns, is impressive from the outside. Its circular murals are a reminder of the tribulations of Clark's successful expedition. Exhibits are on display at the visitor center where a short film about the campaign may be seen.

Near the memorial is the Old Cathedral, also known as St. Francis Xavier Church, which was built in 1826 to replace a log structure. It remains an impressive landmark. The Old Cathedral has the state's oldest library, its orgin dating back to 1794. It is said to contain 10,000 volumes, some of which are as old as the 12th Century.

Vincennes, population 20,000, also is the Knox County seat of government. The courthouse is an imposing, well-maintained limestone structure, its grounds ringed with a wrought iron fence.

A red granite Civil War Memorial at the northeast corner of grounds notes: "In grateful remembrance of the service and sacrifices of the soldiers in the war with the Union, we the people of Knox County have erected this monument." Statues of soldiers stand atop the four corners of the base that supports the memorial's spire.

Across the Wabash River in Illinois is the Lincoln Trails State Memorial, a prelude for what visitors headed east from Illinois on old U.S. 50 will see in the historic old city. It was in this area that Abraham Lincoln and his family are believed to have forded the Wabash en route from Indiana to Illinois in 1830. A bronze figure of Lincoln at the head of a covered wagon marks the spot.

Vincennes is, a city booster claims, "where it all begins." As far as the Northwest Territory is concerned, it is not a great exaggeration. It is, indeed, where it all began.

CHAPTER 8

ILLINOIS

A trace it was called, this route settlers followed as they moved across Indiana and Illinois en route west. Part of U.S. 50, in years to come, would be built in the wagon ruts and in the footprints of those pioneers who left a path through the wilderness that others would follow.

Some settlers stopped along that route in the 1800s, built homes, turned wildernesses into farms and developed small cities and tiny towns that remain as their legacies.

U.S. 50 is a road that reflects a nation not visible on the interstates. It is on this road that the real America can be found.

LAWRENCE COUNTY

The Wabash River divides Indiana and Illinois as it slices past Vincennes on its way south to the Ohio.

Relocated U.S. 50 remains a four-lane divided road, entering Illinois over the Red Skelton bridge. A sign tells visitors: "The People of Illinois Welcome You."

Entrance signs into states, we have learned, vary, each state seeking a phrase that sets it apart from the others. On the opposite side of the river, eastbound travelers are greeted with a "Welcome to Indiana - Crossroads of America" slogan.

The road into Illinois is elevated over the sometimes flooded Wabash Valley bottom lands. Irrigation equipment remains in the fertile fields, a contradiction of nature that requires crops to be watered in hot, dry summers even after the monsoon-like days of wet springs.

There is oil beneath the rich soil. Pumps, their arms rising and falling in constant motion, extract the crude oil from deep in the earth.

Off to the north of U.S. 50 is the Mid-America Air Center, a foreign trade zone. The airport, named George Field for Gen. Harold H. George, was a school for pilots and a training ground for troop carrier missions in World War II. It now is the Lawrenceville municipal airport.

The air center was planned to be a regional hub for freight, but those expectations have yet to be realized although that potential remains.

Once U.S. 50 leaves the valley lowlands it again runs even with the land on each side, no longer elevated above the fields.

Four-lane U.S. 50 ends at Lawrenceville. The old two-lane U.S. 50 business route comes north out of Vincennes, then parallels U.S. 50 as it enters Lawrenceville.

* * *

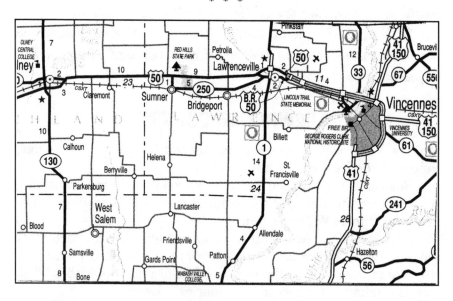

Lawrenceville, a city of 4,900, is the seat of Lawrence County, its courthouse the center of a city in change. Industry is being diversified as an industrial park is developed along U.S. 50 north of the old section of town.

Sometimes lost in the shadow of Vincennes, Lawrenceville is a self-sufficient city with an assortment of businesses, a hospital and an impressive looking high school. Streets are lined with older homes, most of which are well-maintained.

The Embarras (pronounced Ambraw) River slices across the west edge of Lawrenceville on its way south toward its confluence with the Wabash.

* * *

U.S. 50 is again two-lane as it leaves Lawrenceville en route west toward Bridgeport Road that leads a short distance south to the town of Bridgeport, population 2,100.

The new Lawrence County Industrial Park has attracted new industries such as the Daylight Plastics plant. A candy wholesale firm, Rucker's Wholesale and Service, employes about 100 workers.

Red Hills High School, "home of the Salukis," is attended by students from Bridgeport and Sumner, a community to the west. Both towns are on Ill. 250, which in some areas is the route once taken by U.S. 50. The Salukis football teams, as well as the girls basketball teams, have been a source of pride for the community in the late 1990s.

Bridgeport's history dates back to the 1840s. Its churches are old, the pride of citizens deep. Irene Black, who has lived here more than 80 years, called it "the garden spot of the world" in an interview with the "Vincennes Sun-Commercial."

"It has been," she declared, "a community that cared and that has meant a lot. If a community doesn't care, it won't stay a community long."

* * *

The smell of crude oil permeates the car as we drive west. There are oil wells in the area, but the road is lined with scrub land and small fields. The land is not as fertile as it was back toward the river.

Red Hills State Park, the highest point of land between St. Louis and Cincinnati, straddles U.S. 50. It is a good place to find nature as it once was for the 948 acres offers a view of wildflowers and fresh foliage in the spring, the brilliance of nature in the fall when leaves are in full color. Deep ravines, wooded hills and a 40-acre fishing lake are on the grounds that were among the land ceded by Indians to the United States.

Bisecting the park is the old Cahokia Trace, better known as Trace Road, a route taken by settlers on their way west from Vincennes. The route used for Trace Road is a forerunner of U.S. 50.

* * *

To the west a road runs south from U.S. 50 to the city of Sumner, which like its neighbor Bridgeport is on Ill. 250. Unlike some smaller rural towns, it sees progress instead of decline.

That attitude was echoed by Mayor Curtis Dhonau, who told Roger Boyd of the "Vincennes Sun-Commercial:" "We're not just rolling over and playing dead. We're trying to get things going."

Dhonau, a former Vincennes University department head who moved to Sumner in 1988, expects others to follow his move. "People like smaller towns," he says.

Industrial parks in the area are attracting new workers, who may find Sumner an attractive place to live. The nearness of Red Hills State Park makes it an even better option.

RICHLAND COUNTY

Back on U.S. 50, which some officials say may be widened to four lanes, the land is more fertile, the fields larger. The city of Olney is 12 miles to the west.

Off the south side of the road is a cemetery, officially called a "memory garden," with a lake. It is a far different burial site than old pioneer graveyards with tombstones hidden in isolated locations off county roads.

The land is flat, the road straight, lined by big farms and nice homes.

Off to the south is the town of Claremont, population 300. It is another community that owes its birth in 1866 - and much of its existence since - to the railroad it straddles.

It is a farm community, the kind marked by a water tower and a grain elevator, which is busy on this fall day in the midst of the grain harvest. Hog barns and expansive farms surround the town. It is rural America at is best.

* * *

To the west a Mail Pouch tobacco sign is the only paint on a barn that is in disrepair. A house nearby is in excellent condition, a contrast to the past when some farmers maintained barns, but sometimes neglected their homes.

An old section of the road, again called Ill. 250, enters the heart of Olney. U.S. 50 bypassed the town to the south in the mid 1960s.

* * *

Every town has its own source of pride. "Welcome to Olney - Home of the White Squirrel," a sign greets visitors as they enter the town. Drawings of squirrels are on banners that help decorate streets in the business district.

Olney, population 8,700, is the Richland County seat of government, its courthouse on Main Street in its business district.

A new library has replaced the old, which is now the Carnegie Building, home of "Richland County's Treasure Trove of Midwest History and Artifacts. Helping you put knowledge to work." It is good to see an older Carnegie Library still in existence with a new mission.

Unlike in other small towns, a theater, the Arcadia, is still open downtown. A park is not far from downtown, neither is Olney High School where a sign urges "Go Tigers Beat Salem." There are few rivalries more fierce than football and basketball games between neighboring towns in Midwest America.

We note a cross section of American's ethnic diversity at the Hunan Garden, a Chinese restaurant. Workers of Mexican descent bus tables where those of Anglo-Saxon origin have been served by those of Asian backgrounds.

On North West Street, the link between the U.S. 50 bypass and downtown Olney, is Olney Central College, part of the Eastern Illinois Community College District. A wide range of options are available to students - from nursing to physics to training in welding, industrial maintenance, woodworking and other crafts.

A truck terminal and a United Parcel Service is at the intersection of West Street and the U.S. 50 bypass. Also at the intersection is the Holiday Motel (not part of the Holiday Inn Chain) where a 1908 Motel T Ford is on display. The car was built at a time when roads were few and a trip across country was rare.

To the west is a huge Wal-Mart Distribution Center, similar to the one back at U.S. 50 and I-65 at Seymour, Ind. Olney, however, remains a center of farm country. Combines are in fields, waiting for moisture to dry so the harvest can resume.

* * *

U.S, 50 remains straight west of Olney, the land flat and fertile, free of businesses, unsightly billboards and traffic impediments. An old section of the highway is off to the north. So are oil storage tanks.

* * *

Noble, a village of 850, is just north of U.S. 50, nine miles from Olney. It's a farm community with a post office, a market, a cabinet shop, a library, a gift shop and a few other businesses. A restaurant, appropriately called "Country Fare," and a pizza outlet are in town.

It's a small town with its own high school and Village Hall. It is towns such as this that are the real America, where folks care about each other, obey the rules of God and man and follow the work ethic pioneers brought as they cleared the land and expanded the nation.

Back on U.S. 50 the road continues to run straight and level as it moves west past a church and vast farm fields. West of Noble U.S. 250 blends into U.S. 50, but an old section, now an access route, continues to follow the main road.

CLAY COUNTY

A big lumber yard, row-on-row of logs stacked high, awaiting milling, is at the road side. The road crosses Big Muddy Creek, then Little Muddy, as it passes through swamp land. An odor of crude oil again is in the air as U.S. 50 crosses the Little Wabash River.

* * *

Off to the north is Clay City, which gives us another look at small town America. A food mart is at the intersection of U.S. 50 where Main Street enters the town past nice homes and manicured lawns.

Two supermarkets are in town as are a few other stores. If there is a restaurant, we do not find it.

We pass Clay City High School, the town park and a veterans memorial. A sign on a building notes the town's history - "125th year - 1855-1980." It is obvious the 950 residents in Clay City take pride in their town. Other towns should be so fortunate.

A railroad slices through the north edge of Clay City. Its trains are likely to be the only noise to interrupt the serenity of daily life in the town that would be a good place to retire from the traffic and commotion of cities.

* * *

We are in rural southern Illinois, an area of large farms between small communities. A water tower rises on the endless horizon as we approach the city of Flora.

U.S. 50 becomes a four-lane divided route as it circles Flora to the north. An early morning sun glistens against the windows in the South Wire Company factory, a fiery appearance that looks almost unreal. The Flora Industrial Park has had success in attracting new firms to town. The giant John Deere sales business nearby reflects the importance of agriculture to the area.

* * *

Flora's population is listed as 5,500 but it seems to be a much larger city.

Like most towns, businesses have begun to cluster on the bypass. A Pizza Hut, Dairy Queen, Burger King and an ever present Wal-Mart Store are off U.S. 50's main intersection.

A historical marker on the bypass notes the career of Maj. Gen. Lewis B. Parsons who lived in Flora from 1875 until his death in 1907. Parsons was in charge of river and rail transportation for the Army in the Civil War.

Despite the shift of some enterprises out to the bypass, businesses remain in the older areas of Flora, a community of well-kept homes, big churches, civic pride and a few brick streets left over from an earlier era.

As elsewhere, the arrival of the Wal-Mart superstore out on the U.S. 50 bypass had a detrimental effect on downtown Flora. The old section of town no longer is the hub of shopping or a social center where residents congregated on Saturday nights to shop, dine or attend a movie.

All is not lost, however. A new downtown Flora is emerging through the cooperation of city government, Main Street Flora and the Flora Community Development Corporation. It is a community effort, the kind that unites groups for a common good.

And there is still one gathering spot, at least. Our search for local flavor takes us to Grandma's Kitchen in Flora's old section. Twelve pickup trucks are parked outside among a few sedans. "We cook like grandma used to - from scratch," a sign boasts.

Inside, advertisements for town businesses are on display around a wall clock. Most of the tables are occupied. Eight men are at one table, engaging in the type conversations only friends of long standing can enjoy. When a town policeman leaves to patrol the streets, "Dale" - as in "Dale, how are you doing?" - takes his place. The talk continues without interruption. Later another man leaves, and a woman fills the void. The conversation continues as soon as her arrival is acknowledged with "good morning" greetings.

A man, finding a seat at another tables is asked, "How are the bird houses coming?"

The man replies, "Why, do you want to buy one?" It is banter among friends, not the rudeness some visitors unfamiliar with small towns might perceive.

Meantime, a waitress who knows all the customers by name, serves our oatmeal. It is creamy and tasty, the best we've ever tasted, better than we recall back on the farm, better than at the imitation rustic chain restaurants of the 1990s.

We leave "Grandma's Kitchen," feeling better for the harmony we have observed. It is 7 a.m. and people already are checking out items at a yard sale nearby.

Later in the day we enter Flora from the west on old U.S. 50 and drive through the Charley Brown Memorial Park. It is there we meet "Pat" Booth, who without indicating he is the town leader he is, tells us about the park, his pride in it obvious by his comments. Charley Brown, he explains, was a cattle buyer decades ago. His widow, Minnie Brown, gave the land for the park to the town of Flora with the stipulation it would be named in his memory.

The park is three miles from the heart of Flora, a distance some thought might be too great to attract youngsters from town. The kids, Booth adds, have managed to find transportation to the park, which has become one of Flora's bigger assets. It is a rolling wooded area with a swimming pool, picnic grounds and a B&O Railroad caboose called "Little Toot" that is a Kiwanis Club contribution.

Like most men of character, "Pat" Booth gives credit for the park's development - and other facilities in Flora - to others, downplaying his own accomplishments. "Be sure to stop at the library in town," he advises as we leave.

* * *

Back in downtown Flora, the library Booth has mentioned is modernistic, larger than those in some towns 10 times larger in population. Windows provide an openness, unhindered by walls, that give the library a spacious appearance.

Credit Marion Thomas (Sonny) Hall, a noted architect, for the design of library which opened in 1990 when Marcus (Pat)

Expansive public library in downtown Flora

Booth was the Library Board president. It is the same "Pat" Booth with whom we have spoken back at the park.

A woman notes our curiosity as we tour the library and asks: "Are you here for the 1950s reunion?"

It is the weekend when Flora High School graduates of the 1950s are due for a reunion. We have some regret we are not part of the events to unfold within a few hours. It is good to know those who grew up in small towns do not forget their origins.

A veterans' memorial is on the library grounds. On the same block, work is underway on a new City Hall, it, too, designed by architect "Sonny" Hall.

Flora, we conclude, is a small town that appears ready for the 21st Century, confident that its future will exceed its past.

* * *

U.S. 50 is marked as the Blue Star Memorial Highway, a tribute to the Armed Forces that have defended the nation. It is the first time we have seen the Blue Star designation sign since we were back in Indiana.

Salem is 30 miles away as the road cuts slightly to the south-west. No cities are on the route, but we will be surprised at the durability of a couple of small towns along the way.

Four miles to the west, a four-way stop controls traffic at the intersection of Ill. 45, which runs north to the county seat town of Louisville. Another old section of U.S. 50 parallels the new route.

Cattle graze on still green grass. Fields of corn stretch across the horizon on a clear day. Another combine waits for the dew to dry and the harvest to resume. The view is free of unsightly bill-boards. There is little traffic. For a motorists, the livin' is easy.

Harvestore silos rises in the distance, growing larger, like an island at sea, as we grow closer. Not far from grain storage bins are crude oil storage tanks, this being an area where oil and soil are compatible.

* * *

America's greatness comes from the sum of its parts. Some of those parts are the small towns along its highways. Xenia, population 424, is one of those towns that helps give the nation a sense of purpose.

It's a place where a visitor can still see washing on the line, a grain elevator, a square brick house that appears as old as the town.

Xenia, pronounced Zeen'ya, has been a fixture on this route across the nation for decades. It observed its sesquicentennial in 1984, having been platted in 1834 on what was then the Vincennes-St. Louis trail, which is now U.S. 50. The town saw the first train pass through on July 4, 1855, its first stone sidewalk in 1897, its first telephone in 1895. Electric lights went on in town for the first time on July 1, 1901.

The history of the town is told in "Xenia: Then and Now," a comprehensive booklet published for the town's sesquicentennial.

As in other towns, the reason for its name is in dispute. Some think settlers from the east named it for Xenia, Ohio, from which they came. Others contend it was because pioneers considered the area a scenic place and thus named it for a beautiful woman, Princess Xenia of Greece.

Still another story claims residents of the town, the crossing place of two important wagon roads, met to decide on a name at the village tavern. A passing clergyman, said to be "under the mellowing influence of the occasion," explained that Xenia was a Greek word for hospitality and would be an appropriate name."

Being small doesn't keep Xenia from having its own government. Nancy Burkett, a secretary at the Town Hall, tells us Xenia's affairs are run by a mayor and six trustees.

An oil company and a grain elevator are the town's main businesses, but a small factory that makes wire harnessing for cars is out on U.S. 50.

A grade school remains, but older students have attended classes in Flora for decades.

"Is there anything that make Xenia different from other small farm towns? we ask Nancy Burkett.

"Not that I can think of," she replies. Like all towns, however, it has its own personality, its own place in the shaping of a nation. Its sesquicentennial history is proof of that.

MARION COUNTY

The road is narrow as it enters Marion County. Low land along Skillet Fork Creek is lined with trees for a time. Beyond, the creek, work is underway to eliminate a curve on U.S. 50. It is a road on which changes are endless, improvements made in each state as highway budgets allow.

Quickly the terrain changes, the fields grow larger, the soil is again fertile.

* * *

Unlike other small towns across the nation, Iuka, pronounced I-you-ka, is growing. Harold Stevenson, called mayor by some, president of the board of trustees by others, tell us the population is up to about 500, an increase of 50 from an earlier count.

Stevenson has spent most of his life in Iuka, which is incorporated as a village. Government business is conducted by six trustees and the president or mayor, however he is addressed.

"We operate the water and sewer utilities and have one part-time policeman," says Stevenson, who explains how Iuka has changed over the years. Once a farm town, it now is basically a bedroom community for workers who have jobs in Flora or Salem.

A grade school/junior high is in town, but Iuka High School was discontinued after consolidation in 1938.

Penny's Cafe, a breakfast and lunch stop for residents, is in town as are the B & R Grocery, the post office, the Iuka State Bank, an insurance business, a farm sales and service, a funeral home and a beanie baby outlet, beanie babies being an American craze of the late 1990s.

A blacksmith shop is closed, the smithy passing on to his reward, ending an era in the farm community.

A major business is the House of Plunder, a giant store selling merchandise acquired when stores elsewhere went out of business. "This-Is-It" is a business that resells unclaimed clothing bought from dry cleaning shops.

The Fire Department advertises a bean supper, a source of funds which politicians in bigger town would call "revenue enhancement." It appears Iuka is a town that can survive on its own, without depending on Big Brother in Springfield, the state capital, or in Washington, the nation's capital.

* * *

West of Iuka a sign sponsored by a 4-H Club reminds motorists: "Slow Down. Farming Season." It is harvest time in rural Illinois and huge farm equipment is often on the road.

The land is level, the farms large in this land called the Midwest. It is far different than the mountains of West Virginia and we again are awed by the diversity of America that can be seen along this road across the nation on this route called U.S. 50.

Antique tractors are off the road, a nostalgic sales lot for those who remember the John Deeres, Farmalls and Allis Chalmers of the 1940s and 1950s. The historic city of Salem is just ahead.

* * *

A section of Illinois, roughly described as that south of U.S. 50, is known as Little Egypt. It is perhaps for this reason that the state's southernmost city is called Cairo.

The term Little Egypt goes back to the hard and difficult winter of 1830-1831 in the counties to the north. Deep snows came early and stayed late into the spring. Frosts continued into May, delaying the planting seasons, which was short and cool. Crops, which had no time to mature, were ruined when the first killing frost arrived in early September.

Upstate farm families faced a shortage of corn meal, their cattle a lack of feed. They found both in southern Illinois where the weather had been warmer and the devastation less severe.

Farmers, who lived by the words of the Bible, came in wagons to southern Illinois. Like the sons of Jacob, they said, they were going down to Egypt for corn.

They returned with enough to sustains their livestock and to seed another crop, which did not fail. They had been saved by Little Egypt.

And now, 170 years later, the city of Salem sometimes still refers to itself as the "Gateway of Little Egypt."

* * *

Birthplace of William Jennings Bryan

Salem's population is 7,500, but its history is as extensive as some major American cities. A visitor notes the beginning of that heritage at the east edge of the city when he passes the Half-Way Tavern, its name coming from the location a the mid-point between Vincennes and St. Louis.

The tavern, built in 1815 and used as both an inn and livery stable, catered to stagecoach passengers. It was at the Half-Way Tavern that Abraham Lincoln stopped at least once while riding the circuit as a young attorney. The building is not open to the public.

U.S. 50 does not bypass Salem. It instead runs through the heart of the city that is the business center for this area of south central Illinois. It was founded in 1823 as the county seat of Marion County, but it did not become an incorporated village until 1855.

Salem was the home of both William Jennings Bryan, the "silver tongue orator," and, by coincidence, John Thomas Scopes. It was Bryan who spoke at Salem High School's 1919 commencement when Scopes graduated. Six years later the two would face each other, Scopes as the defendant, Bryan as an associate prosecutor in the famous trial in Dayton, Tenn., in which Scopes was charged with teaching the theory of evolution in his high school biology classes.

In that trial, Bryan was opposed by Clarence Darrow, the noted defense attorney. Bryan won the case, Scopes being found guilty and fined $100. It was a costly victory. Bryan died just five days after the trial ended.

Another chapter in Salem's history was written in the 1930s when an oil boom turned some depression-poor farmers wealthy overnight.

Not as fortunate, according to folk lore, was the creator or creators of Miracle Whip. The whip was a recipe - known as Max's X-tra Fine Salad Dressing - used at Max Crossett's Cafe in downtown Salem. The Kraft Company, it is said, bought the recipe in 1931 for $300 and renamed it Kraft's Miracle Whip.

And it was at the American Legion Post in Salem that the G.I. Bill of Rights originated. The Servicemen's Readjustment Act became law on June 22, 1943, to assist World War II veterans return to civilian life once World War II ended.

Much of Salem's history can be observed at the Marion County Courthouse on U.S. 50, where there, too, is concern about the present. Visitors enter the three-story limestone building through a metal detector, a safe guard against guns and weapons. Terrorism and madness is a concern, even here in the heartland of America.

A woman on guard at the walk-through check point reports "a few knives, but no gun," have been detected.

Civil War memorabilia is on the first floor. Marble steps, reflecting construction of an earlier time, leads to the second floor and a 50-foot long mural of "the great commoner," William Jennings Byran, 1860-1925. The mural was dedicated to the American people October 3, 1995. A number of plaques note Bryan's achievements:

Born in Salem, "the common man," Democratic candidate for U.S. president in 1896, 1900 and 1908, secretary of state under President Woodrow Wilson, the man who drafted the 16th to 20th amendments to the constitution, chief prosecutor in Scopes trial.

Also recognized is Francis Marion (1732-1795), for whom the county is named. Marion was the "swamp fox" of the Revolutionary War.

On a quiet street not far from the Courthouse Square is Bryan's birthplace, a modest two-story white home which is now a museum. It is open daily, except Thursdays.

Salem's Chamber of Commerce boasts, "We put the unity into community." It is not an idle slogan, we decided after a few hours in Salem. There is unity here as in other small cities along our route.

* * *

U.S. 50 is three lanes, the center for left turns, as it runs west past a Wal-Mart Store and fast food restaurants. The road widens to four lanes for a short distance at an intersection with north-south I-57.

A farm nearby offers turnips for sale. It is the first time we have seen turnips turned into a cash crop.

The road again narrows to two lanes as it passes a row of houses and a few businesses, which hints Salem may be growing toward the west. A used car lot is at roadside, the only one we remember seeing one on U.S. 50 in Illinois. Traffic stops at a light, which controls traffic one-way through a bridge reconstruction project. Road maintenance is never ending.

* * *

Only short distances separate towns along U.S. 50 in this area of Illinois. Odin, a town of 1,200 residents, is just five miles from Salem to the east, four miles to Sandoval to the west.

Odin is located mostly between the railroad and U.S. 50, a residential town with churches, a police department, a school, a post office, a few businesses, a taxidermy shop and an antique mall.

Pigeons warm in the autumn sun on a roof, oblivious to the traffic on the road.

* * *

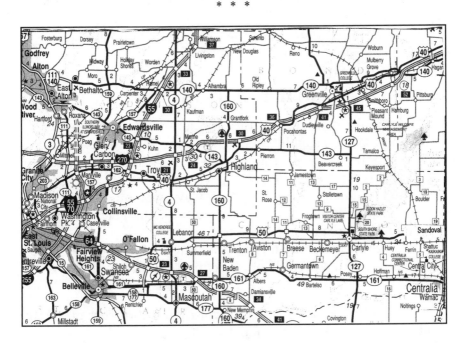

In Sandoval, population 1,500, U.S. 50 stops at U.S. 51, indicating it does not carry as much traffic as north-south U.S. 51. It is here U.S. 50 turns south with U.S. 51 before it makes a 90-degree turn to the west after a short distance.

A restaurant called the "Taylor Maid Drive Inn" is open. So are two taverns with names spouses may resent. One is called "Fat's Rendezvous," the other "The Hide Out."

Sandoval appears to be a residential town with a bank, a few businesses, a post office, a barber shop, beauty salons and a two-story high school painted white, making it different from most of the red ones along the way.

* * *

The road continues through farm country from Sandoval to a crossing of two railroads marked on the road map as Shattuc. A depot remains, but not much else. A sign "Shattuc" near the tracks identifies what once was a railroad stop.

Street names remain, but there are few houses. A dog, lonesome for company, comes out to greet us. Chairs are lined across a porch of one house, indicating Shattuc now is more for relaxation than for business.

We have noted that many towns that grew up with railroads declined with the arrival of the automobile.

CLINTON COUNTY

Huge grain storage facilities appear on the horizon to the west. The road is straight and smooth, the farm houses almost hidden by fields of corn. Grain storage units at one farm cover an area as big as some small towns.

Grain is important to Ferrin, a wide spot on U.S. 50 near where a new grain elevator is being built for the Ferrin Cooperative Equity Exchange.

Other than that, Ferrin is a community of 30 roadside houses and a church with a pre-school for youngsters three to five.

* * *

The land remains fertile, the crops bountiful west of Ferrin about three miles to Huey, population 200.

Tiny post office in town of Huey

Huey is to the south, another town that grew up with the railroad. Clothes are on the line on this Friday now that Monday no longer is the wash day of choice.

At the post office, housed in a tiny 12-by-14-foot building, we meet . Postmaster Linda Jacob. She is alone, most of the day's business having been conducted in the early morning, a time when residents sometimes convene in what doubles as a community center of sorts.

"You're lucky you caught me in," she says, adding, "we close at 1:30 p.m. Tuesdays, Wednesdays and Thursdays, but not until 3:30 on Fridays."

Despite its size, the post office is a full service operation. "We can do everything here that a large post office can do. We just don't have any rural routes," Mrs. Jacob notes.

She took the job, she says, to keep the post office from perhaps closing for lack of a postmaster. An added incentive was the fact Huey, at the time, was home to her in-laws.

"So what happens two days later?," she asks, then answers her own question. "They decide to move away." She laughs at the coincidence.

It's a 50-mile drive from her home in Sparta. "Luckily," she adds, "the Postal Service pays me mileage." Her husband is the postmaster at Baldwin, except when he is sometimes temporarily shifted elsewhere.

"You work for the Postal Service?" she asks, wondering about our curiosity. "Just fascinated with small towns," we explain.

In small towns like Huey, the post office is a social center, Mrs. Jacob agrees. "Five or six people are here each morning talking about the weather, if the soybean crop is in, and whether the corn is ready to harvest. It's a nice community of nice people."

And the post office allows them to buy stamps without having to wait in line at a bigger post office. And to pick up their mail from their own post office box.

It is the kind of place that helps bind a small community. Huey would not be the same without Zip Code 62252.

* * *

A short distance west of Huey is an entrance to the South Shore State Park on the edge of Carlyle Lake, Illinois' largest man-made body of water. The lake was formed in the 1960s when a dam was built across the historic Kaskaskia River.

The lake is smooth, glistening in the sun, reflecting the beauty of a great fall day. A lone sail boat glides across the gentle waves. There are no boats at the ramps, few cars in the parking lot for this is a week day, a time when most folks are at work. What few people there are have a chance to meditate, enjoy the view and to savor the quietude of the moment.

On a sand bar, hundreds of sea gulls strut, proud it seems of their white breasts. A heron prepares to land, its approach even more graceful than an airliner at an airport terminal.

The lake has made Carlyle a destination for those who seek opportunities to fish, sail, hike or picnic.

* * *

Just to the west of the lake on the Kaskaskia River is the city of Carlyle, named for Thomas Carlyle, the Scottish essayist and historian.

Stone abutments anchor Dean Suspension Bridge

U.S. 50 is just south of the famed Dean Suspension Bridge, which brought recognition to Carlyle decades before Carlyle Lake. The bridge has been a landmark since 1861, when it opened as a tribute to American ingenuity and imagination.

Its specifications called for "a sturdy, lasting bridge to span 280 feet from tower to tower." The stone abutments were to reach at least 15 feet, topped by stone towers to be 30-35 feet high.

The bridge served as a major crossing of the Kaskaskia for 65 year, a span crossed by countless Americans on their way west on what was then the Vincennes-St. Louis Road, known also as Goshen Trail.

Spectators, who witnessed some of those crossings, recorded: "The floor seemed to sag like a half moon, and the heavy supporting cables jerked and squeaked under the heavy load when a stampede of 70 cattle crossed the span."

Loads of heavy equipment and materials for oil drilling were transported across the span in 1911 despite its age and the uncertainty of its strength.

The bridge remained open to traffic until 1920 when a more modern span opened 300 feet downstream. Despite its historical significance, the bridge fell into disrepair for years and a piece of Carlyle's past was headed into history. That changed in 1951 when civic pride allowed the structure to be converted to a pedestrian bridge and its one-lane width reduced to six feet.

The action preserved the bridge as a tribute to Gen. William F. Dean in honor of the one-time resident of Carlyle. A small park is at the bridge, which remains open to foot traffic.

We stand on the bridge and enjoy the view, joining a man who identifies himself as Willis Reynolds. He points to wild ducks in the grass; mallards, unafraid of two men fishing nearby.

"Born and raised here," he says. He's aware of the significance of U.S. 50 to Carlyle and to the nation. "Goes all the way to San Francisco," he says proudly. "When I was stationed out there during the war, I'd see U.S. 50 signs and think, 'Man, my home is on that road.'"

As a child he walked across the dilapidated bridge, stepping over missing planks that left gaps that made the journey treacherous but challenging for teen-agers.

The dam changed the area north of the bridge, but Reynolds remembers well those days of his youth. "There was timber there," he says, pointing north. "I hunted squirrels back in those woods many times. He eyes a sandbar. "That's where I learned to swim, over in that old river bed."

Reynolds likes Carlyle. "It is like home. Nice and quiet," he says, not like St. Louis where he lived for five years.

"I couldn't take that city (St. Louis) any longer. I wanted to come back where I was born and raised and bring my children back here to grow up." The return to his roots meant he had to commute 54 miles each way to his job in St. Louis. Two hours a day on the road were a small price to pay for the joy of being back home.

"Now that I am retired I can fish and hunt," he says, a hint of satisfaction in his voice.

We leave him to his bridge and his town. It is good to see a citizen who is proud of his surroundings and happy with his station in life.

Another man removes fishing gear from his car. He doesn't much care, he says, what kind of fish he catches. The relaxation is more important. "Oh, I like to catch carp once in a while, but you have to wait them out like any other kind of fish."

He has driven up from Okawville, about 25 miles away. That's not too far, he says. The enjoyment of a leisurely day at river's edge will pay for the drive.

* * *

Carlyle is the seat of government of Clinton County, one of the few rural Illinois counties that has shown a population gain each decade in the 1900s. A new brick and stone courthouse is nearing completion on the square along U.S. 50 as the county prepares for the new millennium.

The past, however, will not be forgotten. A memorial remains. "Dedicated to veterans of Clinton County who served their country with honor and distinction and made the supreme sacrifice," it reads.

Businesses are open on the streets surrounding the Courthouse, activity brisk for a town of 3,200 residents. Across the street, Patrick's Restaurant offers excellent food amid a peaceful atmosphere. A long bar faces a mirrored wall. The bar, the kind that once was a fixture in taverns, is a carryover from the 1930s, a waitress explains.

This is a proud town. A sign notes that the high school is home of the Carlyle Indians. "Welcome to Carlyle - Titletown - State Champs - football 1981, basketball 1989, 1996, 1997," it boasts.

The spire at St. Mary's Church rises over the flat lands surrounding Carlyle, a guide of sorts for the lost.

Riddel's Court, a motel that is a reminder of the old tourist cabins of the past, is open. So are two other motels, Sunset Motel and Motel Carlyle, but no national motels have come to the city. That's not true for superstores. A Wal-Mart Discount City is at west edge of Carlyle on old U.S. 50.

* * *

The old U.S. 50 route west out of Carlyle is connected via 12th Street to a new 22-mile section of U.S. 50, just over a mile north of town, that extends west to Lebanon.

We continue on the old route a short distance to the town of Beckemeyer, population 1,100. Beckemeyer, which appears to be mostly a residential town, has joined the search for an expanded tax base. An industrial park is near the town, which has a police force. The up-to-date Beckemeyer-Wade Township Fire Department has its own home page on the Internet and lets other departments know it can provide them with their own web sites. Rural communities no longer are out of touch with the world beyond.

* * *

West of Beckemeyer, the road is elevated over the Shoal Creek lowlands, guard rails separating motorists from trees on each side. A few miles later the road again is even with the fields on each side.

* * *

Every town has its own motto. Signs at the entrance to Breese, population 3,500, note it is "Famous For Friendliness." A Lion's Club member proves the point. He is at an intersection of old U.S. 50 and a busy Breese street, trading mints for donations on Lions Club Candy Day.

In small towns, service clubs are the glue that cements civic endeavors, their members volunteers in community efforts.

"Is this Breese with an 's' or a 'z'?" we ask the Lion.

"Breese with a 's' - like Mariah, the wind," he laughs, thanking us for the contribution to the causes of Lionism.

No matter its name, Breese is a breathe of fresh air, a neat, clean town. The water tower is decorated with leaves on tree branches as if ruffled by a gentle breeze. Similar emblems can be seen in town.

The Mater Dei Catholic High School proclaims it is "home of the Knights." "Cougar Country" notes a sign at Central Community High School, which is at the edge of town.

Not far away is an ideal small town park with playgrounds, picnic areas, shelter houses, a swimming pool, basketball court and hockey rink.

Streets in Breese are wide and well-maintained. If there is unsightliness in Breese we do not see it.

* * *

Village Hall in town of Aviston

We return to open country, but only for a short time. The march of towns continue as another tall church spire shows the way west over the prairie into Aviston, population 1,000.

"Aviston, established in 1864, welcomes you," a sign reads. Compared to cities and towns back east on U.S. 50, Illinois towns are young, growing up as the population moved west in the last half of the 1800s.

Aviston is named for John Avis, a gunsmith who owned the area's first business in the early 1800s. The town, however, did not flourish until the 1860s when the B&O Railroad opened, bringing with it a depot, passengers and freight.

Trees line the streets, one appropriately named Elm, as old U.S. 50 passes through town. The post office is in what appears to have been a house. Town government is based in the brick Village Hall, which has a bell house atop the roof of the old building. It is another town linked to the railroad that runs through it.

At St. Francis Catholic Church, grade school children use their physical education period to play kickball. St. Francis Community Park adjoins the school grounds.

An old two-story house with a metal roof and windows across the front appears to anchor the small town. It is old, but in good repair, proof that deterioration does not necessarily come with age.

Another of the older homes is in disrepair, but its condition does not hide its history. A detached two-bay garage at the side appears to have once been a place for carriages instead of autos.

* * *

The terrain changes from flat to rolling west of Aviston. A well is being drilled near a new housing addition, indicating the possibility of another suburban development for those who wish to commute to jobs in St. Louis. The project is in contrast to another giant grain storage facility nearby, an indication a blend of farms and housing units may be in the area's future.

Up ahead is Trenton, population 2,500. A park is at the town's east side, a place to play in contrast to a cemetery nearby.

A banner on old U.S. 50 notes Trenton is "A Growing Place, A Place to Grow." The Chamber of Commerce touts Trenton as "A good place to visit - a nice place to work - a great place to live."

Trenton began as a dream in 1836 when A. W. Casad laid out a town and called it Trenton for his home back in New Jersey. No homes were built, however, and there was little development until the 1850 when a railroad depot and post office opened and the town was replatted. A village charter was granted in 1856 and in 1887 Trenton was incorporated as a city.

A modern town hall is open, so are some businesses. In the city park are a swimming pool, baseball diamonds, playgrounds, basketball courts and soccer fields. Two grade schools are in Trenton; the Wesclin school district high school is three miles to the south on Ill. 160.

* * *

We have noticed that Illinois towns, too small for Wal-Marts, have Casey General Stores, more like the convenience stores of today than the general stores of the mid-1900s.

ST. CLAIR COUNTY

We return to farm country west of Trenton as we enter St. Clair County. Two semitrailers wait in a field as another pulls out onto the highway en route to a grain elevator, an indication of the productivity of the land.

Up ahead is the farm community of Summerfield, a wide spot in the road, smaller than its neighbors back to the east.

Old U.S. 50 merges with the new section as the road follows its old route into Lebanon. A scenic view is before us as a ridge rises on the horizon to the west.

* * *

On the 22-mile drive on old U.S. 50 from Carlyle, we have passed through five towns, each with reduced speed limits. The new route to the north has speeded traffic but isolated the communities from motorists in a rush to the west or to the east. It has been an advantage for those who commute from Carlyle and other towns to jobs in St. Louis.

But for every winner there is a loser. The loss is a part of America which has been left behind, no longer seen by travelers who prefer the quickest route between two points.

We travel the new section from west-to-east later. It passes through prime land and big farms. Five huge dairy farms are on the road between Breese and Carlyle, the operators harvesting corn between milkings.

It is a chance for travelers to see the agricultural importance of the bread basket of America.

* * *

Once again, a spire and water tower rise in the distance as we cross Silver Creek into Lebanon. The Fall Festival is about to start and the city of 3,700 is dressed for the occasion. "Welcome to Historic Lebanon," a greeting says.

It is a an old town with lots of oak, maple and other hardwood trees and big houses, two of which offer bed and breakfast. The Landmark on Madison, circa 1906, has a circular porch. Across the street is the Queen Ann, established in 1902.

A "Beautify Lebanon Area" is at a main intersection on U.S. 50, a sign noting it was a winner of the governor's hometown award in a "Building Illinois With Volunteers" program. Some streets remained paved in brick.

U.S. 50 runs through the heart of Lebanon, passing the Mermaid House and other historic buildings. At a main intersection, as back in Breese, Lions Club members are trading mints for donations to finance their community efforts.

* * *

It is at the Mermaid House we meet Helen Church, a delightful lady, who shares the significance of the Lebanon landmark.

English novelist Charles Dickens, she explains, was among a group of investors in southern Illinois land. Dickens and others, concerned about the amount of return on their investments, came to the area in 1842. After a stop in St. Louis, the 14-man group came to Lebanon in a wagon train for a closer look at the American prairie that had interested Dickens.

The Mermaid House was their overnight stop. "It was larger, then, with a lot more rooms," says Mrs. Church.

But why is it called Mermaid House?

Mrs. Church laughs, then replies:

"The closest water we have is Silver Creek, yet the hotel is called the Mermaid House. Lyman Adams, a retired sea captain, called it that when he opened the hotel in the 1830s, confessing he believed in mermaids after having seen them at sea." Mrs. Church pauses a minute, then adds:

Mermaid House on U.S. 50 in Lebanon

"We think he may have imbibed too much while at sea."

Antiques dating back to the early 1800s, some donated by Mrs. Church, are on display in the house which has hand-hewn oak beams, held in place by wooden pegs. A small section of plaster has been removed to reveal the original lathes and the beams.

The Church family has long been associated with Lebanon's history. It was Leon Church who founded the Lebanon Historical Society. And it was Leon Church who helped save the Indian mounds northeast of town, which were turned over to the state of Illinois in 1973.

Mrs. Church is a town treasure, an asset as valuable as the Mermaid House. As with all historical groups, volunteers are few. If there were more, Mrs. Church says, she wouldn't be the hostess as often as she is. "I'm just too old to do it well," she says, laughing again.

She is too modest. Lebanon is a small city in which residents can take pride. People like Helen Church make it so.

* * *

Not far from downtown Lebanon is McKendree College, the first college established in Illinois and the oldest in the nation with continuous ties to the Methodist Church.

It was established as the Lebanon Seminary in 1828 by pioneer Methodists, becoming McKendree College in 1830 with permission granted by William McKendree, the first American-born bishop of the Methodist Church.

Its curriculum is much broader now as students prepare for the 21st Century by choosing from among 31 areas of study in which they may earn degrees.

* * *

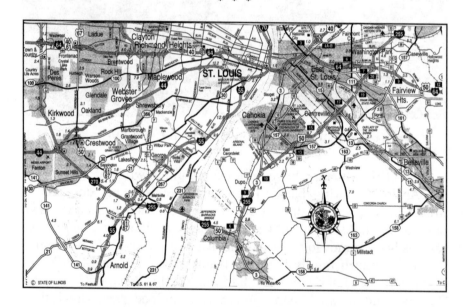

From Lebanon, U.S. 50 dips to the southwest through some scrub lands, the speed limit seldom more than 50 mph. The route joins Interstate 64 on a northwesterly route through the town of O'Fallon on its way toward St. Louis less than 20 miles away.

At Washington Park, it joins I-255, on a southwestern route around St. Louis before crossing the Mississippi into Missouri.

The small towns and cities we have passed through since leaving Cincinnati are gone. We are in the suburbs of St. Louis. The fields and farmlands have disappeared, urban sprawl has begun.

At intersections, open spaces have disappeared, and trees have been uprooted, huge shopping malls are growing where corn once flourished. Unlike small towns, the cluster of growth at the quadrants of the interchanges look much the same. Motels, fast food outlets, the chain steakhouses and department stores are the same off one interstate ramp as at another. In many subdivisions, one house looks like another, a place for families to live for a time, then move on to wherever a mobile job market calls. It is a far different era than the mid-1800s when families moved into Illinois, put down roots, developed farms and stayed, one generation after another.

The gentle character of the road behind has disappeared. Like traffic, life moves faster, there is little time to enjoy the land beyond the road. Exits lead to suburbs without focal points. The spirit and harmony that unite old established towns are threatened. It is progress with a price.

* * *

U.S. 50 accompanies I-255 to the southwest, then crosses the Mississippi River, turns north around southwest St. Louis to join I-44. Beyond the city of Union, it turns west to begin its journey toward San Francisco.

POSTSCRIPT

Our journey along "The Forgotten Highway" has covered more than 900 miles and taken us to 130 cities and towns in six states. It has been a fascinating trip across a part of America most travelers never see.

We have taken a road far different than the interstates where motorists check in at motels, eat at fast-food restaurants, stay a few hours and depart, oblivious to where they are and what is beyond the billboard and chain link fences.

Interstates are for speed. U.S. 50 is to enjoy and to view life on the slow lanes. Each mile is different than the one left behind or the one ahead. The road rises and falls like a rollercoaster; coils and turns like a cow path, runs straight like the path of an archer's arrow.

It has taken us to the grandeur of Virginia's horse country, the simple charm of West Virginia mountain towns, the scenic terrain of southern Ohio, the gentle hills of Indiana and the vast farm lands of Illinois.

But it is the people - from mayors to junk dealers - that most impressed us. We found them in village stores, post offices, cafes and at roadside markets; real people with little pretense, but with an abundance of honesty, courtesy and friendliness.

It is on this road that winds over rivers and brooks, through valleys, over mountains, into small towns and cities and across farm lands that the heritage of cultures blend into a nation of people called Americans.

It is a trip that will uplift the spirit and renew faith in the goodness of the USA.

THE AUTHOR

"The Forgotten Highway" is Wendell Trogdon's sixteenth book, each of which had its origin in his native Indiana.

Trogdon retired in 1962 as managing editor of "The Indianapolis News" after a 38 year newspaper career. He has continued as a columnist for "The News" and other publications.

Among his works are a series of five nostalgia books about life in rural southern Indiana in the 1930s and 1940s. Five others are about high school basketball, Indiana's game, as seen from the viewpoints of referees, coaches, players and fans.

In addition to "The Forgotten Highway," he is the author of two other travel books. "Backroads Indiana" is a journal of his travels over unbeaten paths to small, isolated southern Indiana towns. "Borderline Indiana" is a look at the people and places along the 1,000-mile border that shapes the Hoosier State.

He also is the author of "Indiana General Stores/Vanishing Landmarks," which includes his visits to 100 old rural stores that remain despite competition from the Wal-Marts, Lowe's and Furrows of today.

The author resides at Mooresville, Ind., with his wife, Fabian, who took the pictures in this book. They may be reached by mail at P.O. Box 651, Mooresville, IN 46158 or by e-mail at wend@iquest.net.

Correction: The author retired from *The Indianapolis News* in 1992, not 1962.

INDEX